Southern Literary Studies
Fred Hobson, Editor

Pastoral and Politics in the Old South

Pastoral and Politics in the Old South

JOHN M. GRAMMER

Louisiana State University Press
Baton Rouge and London

Copyright © 1996 by Louisiana State University Press
Manufactured in the United States of America
First printing
05 04 03 02 01 00 99 98 97 96   5 4 3 2 1

Designer: Michele Myatt
Typeface: Goudy
Typesetter: Impressions Book and Journal Services, Inc.
Printer and binder: Thomson-Shore, Inc.

Library of Congress Cataloging-in-Publication Data

Grammer, John M., 1957–
    Pastoral and politics in the old South / John M. Grammer.
       p.   cm. — (Southern literary studies)
    Includes bibliographical references and index.
    ISBN 0-8071-2117-7 (cloth : alk. paper)
    1. Southern States—Intellectual life—19th century.   2. American
literature—Southern States—History and criticism.   3. American
literature—1783–1850—History and criticism.   4. Southern States—
Civilization—1775–1865.   I. Title.   II. Series.
F213.G72   1997
975'.03—dc20   96-22786
                                                                               CIP

The paper in this book meets the guidelines for permanence and durability
of the Committee on Production Guidelines for Book Longevity of the Council
on Library Resources. ∞

For Elizabeth

For my father, John C. Grammer, Jr.

To the memory of my mother, Jessica Turpin Grammer

CONTENTS

Acknowledgments

Though the writing of this book spanned several years and two states, I have found myself continually surrounded by wise and generous friends, and I wish to express my gratitude to them. At the University of Virginia, Stephen Arch, Deborah Garfield, Anne MacMaster, Catherine Wilcoxson Parrish, and Monica Brzezinski Potkay all offered helpful advice. Also at Virginia, J. C. Levenson, Edward Ayers, and especially Alan Howard read the manuscript with critical eyes and made valuable suggestions. John Ernest, best of graduate school friends, spent many hours with me and my book, arguing and encouraging, and in the years since we left Charlottesville, he has been tireless in urging me to get the thing in final form and in print—for all of which I offer heartfelt thanks.

At the University of the South I have been similarly fortunate. John Willis promptly and thoroughly answered every historical question I asked him and alerted me to valuable sources. The incomparable Mariana Johnson was of enormous help in preparing the index. Woody Register, most collegial of colleagues, offered prudent counsel at one crucial turn and friendship, commiseration, and wry irony throughout. The late Edwin Murdoch Stirling, the English Department chairman who hired me, never read a word of this book, but he did everything else imaginable to make me and Elizabeth feel at home in Sewanee and provided as well an example of teaching as a moral commitment that continues to inspire me. And I hardly know where to begin thanking Wyatt Prunty, who nagged me until I finally showed him my manuscript, read it, pronounced it publishable, and then nagged me some more until I submitted it to the press. Every brand-new professor should be blessed with such a mentor.

Lewis Simpson read an unsolicited manuscript from a complete stranger with extraordinary care and offered much useful advice; Fred Hobson did the same for Louisiana State University Press, and the finished product is richer for their suggestions. I thank them both for their kindness. Through the whole business my greatest debt has been to David Levin, exemplary elder and dear friend. He directed my work with wit, tact, patience, and generous encouragement, and in these early years of my teaching career he has been a mentor, adviser, and above all a model of what a scholar and teacher ought to be. As all his former students know, he sets us a formidable example of integrity, open-mindedness, and unfailing kindness.

There are no words to thank Elizabeth Elkin Grammer. Having come into my life only as I was completing this book, she bears little responsibility for its final shape. But for the shape of my life itself, which she has altogether transformed, I owe her everything.

Pastoral and Politics
in the Old South

INTRODUCTION

In his *Reveries over Childhood and Youth*, W. B. Yeats recalls a time when, deep in youthful idealism, he supposed that he as a modern artist would be able to achieve a unity with his native Irish culture and thus become its true spokesman. He imagined that high art in general, poetry in particular, "should be a Centaur finding in the popular lore its back and its strong legs." But in time he came to regard this unity as impossible: "I did not foresee, not having the courage of my own thought," he writes, "the growing murderousness of the world." He then quotes his own most famous lines: "The best lack all conviction, while the worst / Are full of passionate intensity."[1] Thus defeated by the violence, the vulgarity, the ideological passions of his Ireland, the chastened Yeats found that he could not write of it and for it. Instead he retreated into imagination, including, particularly, an imaginary Ireland, one his art could celebrate and make articulate. Thus a poem like "The Fisherman," in which the poet, having faced the bitter impossibility of writing "for my own race," stumbles upon the expedient of "imagining a man" as the subject of his poem—an ideal, representative, "wise and simple" Irishman, clad in gray Connemara cloth, deftly casting his flies in the dawn light. This hero is, as Yeats concedes, "a man who does not exist"; he is nonetheless the only worthy subject available to a national poet writing in debased times.[2]

It is an odd procedure, perhaps, to begin a study of antebellum south-

---

1. William Butler Yeats, *Reveries over Childhood and Youth*, in *The Autobiography of William Butler Yeats* (New York, 1953), 117–18.
2. William Butler Yeats, *Collected Poems* (New York, 1979), 145–46.

ern literature by quoting Yeats. But the problem he articulates in "The Fisherman" and elsewhere is a difficulty faced not just by modern Irish poets but by any writer attempting to speak on behalf of his culture. It states particularly well the situation of the five southern thinkers— John Taylor, John Randolph, Nathaniel Beverley Tucker, George Fitzhugh, and Joseph Glover Baldwin—with whom I am concerned here. All of them aspired to speak for their region, and all of them, sooner or later, found that they had to begin by reinventing it.

Nor, of course, were the troubles of Yeats's time and place unique: the best have lacked conviction, and the worst have overflowed with intensity, more than once in modern times. In American culture that moment of destructive crisis, together with the poet's suspicion that order could be maintained only in language, may have come most notably during the years of social dislocation and sectional conflict which led up to the Civil War. Writers and intellectuals on both sides of the conflict, seeing the American Union and the world-historical promise it claimed to represent on the verge of self-destruction, attempted in art to offer some image of wholeness and recovery. One may think of Ralph Waldo Emerson's ideal "American Scholar," or Harriet Beecher Stowe's Quaker household, or even Nathaniel Hawthorne's Puritans as images of a better America, offered to a troubled nation at a troubled time. "Who except myself," Walt Whitman asked his country, "has yet conceived what your children en-masse really are?"[3] He was claiming for himself a mission to which many American writers felt called. This book examines a less familiar aspect of that literary project: it traces the efforts of five Virginians, during the troubled years of the sectional conflict, to offer to their country an image of social virtue and wholeness—an image they gradually learned to call "the South."

Few readers nowadays will be surprised to hear that the South is as much a concept as it is a place and that the process of constructing the idea of the South was essentially a literary one. Like America itself, the South was written into existence, first by the pamphleteers of the

---

3. Walt Whitman, "Long, Too Long, America," in *Walt Whitman: Complete Poetry and Collected Prose* (New York, 1982), 445.

Virginia Company, who promised economic opportunity and easy living to Englishmen who could be induced to leave their native land, and later by American statesmen on whom it slowly dawned that the tobacco-growing and slaveholding section of the country had developed its own set of political and economic interests. By the time of the Missouri crisis of 1819–1820, it was becoming common for Americans to refer to that section as "the South."

But the region was large and diverse, and growing more so all the time. As hapless Confederate politicians were to discover during the Civil War, the South was at best a highly unstable combination, displaying notable centrifugal tendencies; at worst it seemed hardly more than a legal fiction. The Confederacy, said Karl Marx, was not a nation but a battle cry.

Thus for the southern writers who began trying in the 1820s to discover or create a principle of unity that would give coherent meaning to the South, the difficulties were considerable. Not the least of these was that they undertook this intellectual labor for the sake of an audience that remained largely indifferent to their efforts. The lack of an intellectual culture in their region, the scarcity of readers, and the poverty of their taste are the laments of nearly all southern writers during the thirty years before the Civil War. Many of them responded by adopting the romantic stance of the artist as outcast, cultivating a sense of isolation from philistine surroundings.[4] Thus they found themselves in roughly the situation of Ireland's Yeats, needing to speak for their people yet feeling at times that these people were hardly worth the trouble. Accordingly, these southerners sometimes felt compelled to retreat inward; they were tempted, like Yeats, by the expedient of "imagining a man."

But they seldom rested comfortably in that posture of romantic isolation. In fact, only a handful of southern writers—Edgar Allan Poe is the chief example—really regarded themselves as artists in quite the modern sense, the sense Charles Baudelaire had in mind when he declared that "the man of letters is the world's enemy." For the South

---

4. See Drew Gilpin Faust, *The Sacred Circle: The Dilemma of the Intellectual in the Old South, 1840–1860* (Baltimore, 1977).

preserved, longer than other sections of the country, the antique idea of the man of letters as public man, with public responsibilities; and these responsibilities became increasingly acute as the sectional crisis intensified. "We want above all things a Southern literature," said John C. Calhoun in 1847, "from school books up to the works of the highest order." "It is all important that we should write our own books," added the Virginian George Fitzhugh; "it matters little who makes our shoes."[5] Nor were the responsibilities of the writer limited to literary and forensic exertions; the South retained a touching faith in the abilities of its writers in purely practical matters as well. When Charleston found itself imperiled by Yankee fleets during the Civil War, the city's leaders found it no more than natural to engage the energetic novelist William Gilmore Simms to design coastal defenses. (Simms complied, by the way, and did a creditable job.) This same Simms was a state legislator, trusted counselor of the governor, and narrowly missed being elected lieutenant governor. Like most male southern authors, including the five Virginians I discuss in the following pages, he was a lawyer. This vocational choice was a significant one, as Robert Ferguson has shown in his study of law and literature in America. Ferguson argues that a "Configuration of Law and Letters"—the only literary flourish a young republic could allow itself—dominated American literary culture throughout the Early National period and persisted in the South, as nowhere else, well beyond the Civil War.[6]

Southern writers, then, did more than tinker with ideas when they sought to isolate the essence of southern identity; they fulfilled social responsibilities as they saw them. If part of their task was private, imaginative, and therefore "modern," then another part was public, rhetorical, archaic. Southern writers thought of themselves as leaders, and they required followers. Thus they felt constrained to make their conceptions palatable to the unruly people whom they sought to corral

5. John C. Calhoun, quoted in Louis D. Rubin, Jr., *The Edge of the Swamp: A Study in the Literature and Society of the Old South* (Baton Rouge, 1989), 12; George Fitzhugh, "Southern Thought," in *The Ideology of Slavery: Proslavery Thought in the Antebellum South, 1830–1860*, ed. Drew Gilpin Faust (Baton Rouge, 1981), 279.

6. Robert A. Ferguson, *Law and Letters in American Culture* (Cambridge, Mass., 1984).

within the term *southern*. Those people had, of course, certain ingrained social, political, and economic habits, and the writers who sought to define them must take some account of these. Some theorists of southern identity managed to treat the preexisting cultural realities of their region as valuable raw material for the construction of regional identity; others found those realities, or some of them, to be obstacles to the fulfillment of their designs, insubordinate local facts that must be absorbed or vanquished by some imperial idea of the South. The Virginia author and politician John Taylor used to speak of the great pleasure of "fitting ideas to substances, and substances to ideas."[7] Not all southern writers would have agreed about the pleasure involved, but most were attempting the same negotiation between those two realms—the realms, as we might say, of mind and history.

What was there to bind southerners together within a single regional identity? Slavery, of course, gave them at least the sense of having something in common, particularly after the institution had become embattled. But the peculiar institution was in certain ways a poor rallying cry, for it was an institution with which southerners themselves in the past had often been uncomfortable. The region's intellectual heritage regarding slavery consisted of more criticism than apologia. As Larry Tise has shown, proslavery thought in America, until the 1830s, was largely a New England export, an aspect of the hierarchical politics of high Federalism. Between 1790 and 1840, Tise argues, antislavery activity was more likely to originate in the South than in the North.[8] Thus slavery, though eventually some came to regard it as the proper foundation of southern thought, seemed in the early days of regional self-consciousness rather unpromising raw material.

And there was agriculture, of course; throughout the antebellum period the South remained much more agrarian than the Northeast. This was a difference that made a difference, as one of the earliest

7. John Taylor, *Arator, Being a Series of Agricultural Essays, Practical and Political, in Sixty-Four Numbers,* ed. M. E. Bradford (Indianapolis, 1977), 313.

8. Larry E. Tise, *Proslavery: A History of the Defense of Slavery in America, 1701–1840* (Athens, Ga., 1987).

episodes of sectional tension, the Nullification crisis in South Carolina, made plain: protective tariffs, good for manufacturers and bad for farmers, were nearly as potent a source of regional tension as slavery. But the southern spokesmen I consider, though they took economic interests seriously, were seldom content to let the southern identity seem a mere matter of protecting profits. Especially as the northern moral critique of slavery began to gather force, southern spokesmen wanted a moral issue of their own on which to stake their claim. Agriculture as a mere business interest did not suffice.

The nearest thing the southern region had to a collective myth of identity was a rather loose cluster of ideas, traditions, and symbols which in the following pages I call "pastoral republicanism."[9] The first component of the term is perhaps understood well enough, though I will have a bit to say about it shortly. As for the second, we have only fairly recently had the wherewithal to comprehend its full meaning. Beginning in the mid-1960s, with studies by Bernard Bailyn, Gordon Wood, J. G. A. Pocock, and others, historians have been developing an understanding of the body of thought which Pocock has called "the Atlantic Republican Tradition." They have taught us, first, that republicanism was a tremendously powerful cultural influence in America, providing the symbolic vocabulary employed by most political and social thinkers, North and South, from the time of the Revolution until that of the Civil War. And they have shown that this body of thought was a great deal more than a political theory; it offered its adherents a comprehensive account of human life in society, including theories of history, economics, social life, and personal morality. These historians have traced the central themes of Anglo-American republicanism forward from the radical seventeenth-century critics of the Stuart kings— John Milton, James Harrington, Algernon Sidney, and others—to the eighteenth-century Opposition or "Country" party and its critique of Robert Walpole and the Robinocracy, and at last to colonial America, where it formed the intellectual core of revolutionary rhetoric. Other historians, following those themes as they were developed in the new

9. Robert E. Shalhope coins this term in his *John Taylor of Caroline: Pastoral Republican* (Columbia, S.C., 1980).

nation, have found them pervasively at work in American political thought and rhetoric throughout the antebellum period.[10]

What was Anglo-American republicanism? Pocock summarizes it succinctly as "a civic and patriot ideal in which the personality was founded in property, perfected in citizenship, but perpetually threatened by corruption, government figuring paradoxically as the principal source of corruption and operating through such means as patronage, factions, standing armies (opposed to the ideal of the militia), established churches (opposed to Puritan and deist modes of American religion), and the promotion of a monied interest."[11] The republican persuasion was founded in a distrust of power and an insistence on human liberty. But this preoccupation led in a variety of directions. As a theory of history, republicanism—because it supposed that governments by their nature coveted power and that citizens would always

10. See, for instance, H. Trevor Colbourn, *The Lamp of Experience: Whig History and the Intellectual Origins of the American Revolution* (Chapel Hill, 1965); Bernard Bailyn, *The Ideological Origins of the American Revolution* (Cambridge, Mass., 1967); Gordon S. Wood, *The Creation of the American Republic, 1776–1787* (Chapel Hill, 1969); J. G. A. Pocock, *Politics, Language and Time: Essays on Political Thought and History* (New York, 1971), and *The Machiavellian Moment: Florentine Political Thought and the Atlantic Republican Tradition* (Princeton, 1975); Lance Banning, *The Jeffersonian Persuasion: Evolution of a Party Ideology* (Ithaca, 1978). The "republican synthesis" of Bailyn and his followers has now begun to be challenged, mainly by defenders of the old idea (associated with scholars such as Richard Hofstadter and Louis Hartz) that liberalism constitutes the principal ideology of America. Representative of this attack is Joyce Appleby, *Liberalism and Republicanism in the Historical Imagination* (Cambridge, Mass., 1992). But even scholars who believe that America was never a truly republican political order, or that it ceased to be one shortly after the Revolution, will usually grant the point I argue here, that the symbolic vocabulary of republicanism remained dominant throughout the antebellum period. The best accounts of the rise and partial fall of the republican synthesis may be found in a pair of essays by Robert E. Shalhope, "Toward a Republican Synthesis: The Emergence of an Understanding of Republicanism in American Historiography," *William and Mary Quarterly*, 3rd ser., XXIX (1972), 49–80, and "Republicanism and Early American Historiography," *William and Mary Quarterly*, 3rd ser., XXXIX (1982), 334–56; and in a later one by Daniel Rodgers, "Republicanism: The Career of a Concept," *Journal of American History*, LXXIX (1992), 11–38.

11. Pocock, *Machiavellian Moment*, 507.

be hard-pressed to restrain them—tended toward gloom. It had what amounted to a theory of entropy, a belief that republican societies generally tended toward tyranny and that only a virtuous citizenry, always ready to turn the nation back toward its republican traditions, could interrupt that tendency. Because government tended over time to become tyrannical, time itself could seem an enemy of republican order. History—the realm of time and change—could appear the ultimate tyrant, ordaining the defeat of the republic. One of Pocock's great contributions has been to focus attention on the epiphanic moment when the republic confronts this tyranny—confronts the fact of its ultimate finitude in time: the Machiavellian moment, he calls it, sixteenth-century Florence offering a paradigmatic instance of this confrontation. Because of its historical view, republican utterance could take the form of apocalyptic prophecy, interpreting every mishap as a sign of the republic's impending demise. Or it could take the nearly opposite form of millennialism, a wish to theorize some radical social transformation that would permit an ultimate escape from history and its destructive cycles. Or—perhaps most commonly—it could become a kind of functional pessimism, involving both an expectation that things will tend to go wrong and a determination to remain vigilant and resist this degenerative tendency. All these versions of the republican historical vision may be found at work in antebellum America, North and South.

As a theory of social and personal morality, republicanism tended to create a Manichaean universe in which virtuous citizens and corrupt rulers faced each other across an unbridgeable chasm. Virtue consisted mainly of independence, a will and an ability to resist the power of government—both its power to coerce and its power to seduce. Virtue involved physical and moral courage (the willingness to bear arms for the republic was an important component), a capacity for stern self-denial, and a constant attention to one's public duty. Vice involved all the opposite traits, traits that would make the citizen susceptible to power: not just cowardice but sloth, love of luxury, and selfishness. The long sectional debate in America, of course, echoed and reechoed with these terms, as northerners and southerners charged one another with lapses of republican virtue which threatened the survival of the nation.

As a political theory republicanism was what we would now call a strategy for the unmasking of ideology—ideology in the Marxist sense of class interest masquerading as universal truth: *Tyranny Unmasked*, John Taylor's 1821 attack on protective tariffs, differs from other republican texts only in naming their common enterprise a bit more explicitly than most. A republican thinker, with his ingrained suspicion of power, was always prepared to see some selfish interest at work behind the most noble-seeming ideals: the sovereignty of the English king, or the authority of the federal government, or the sacredness of the Union. As a social theory, republicanism, because of the high value it placed on the economic independence of the citizen, made landed property an important component, and eventually a symbolic representation, of virtue. And correlatively, because it feared the co-option of the government by selfish minorities, republicanism could be intensely suspicious of the small but powerful commercial and manufacturing classes of the country. This component of republican thought was of course particularly agreeable to the agrarian South but may be observed at work in the North—in the rhetoric of the Free Soil party, for instance—as well.

If northerners, too, were deeply affected by republican thought, also using its terms to interpret the sectional conflict, we may question whether it is meaningful to discuss southern republicanism as a distinct category of thought. I believe it is, and in fact I am inclined to believe that we can encounter republicanism only in its various local incarnations; "pure republicanism" is a useful abstraction but not a thing we are likely to glimpse in reality. One recalls Clifford Geertz's argument about the cultural function of ideology: that it is a form of "symbolic action" by which certain anxieties and discontents may be expressed.[12] An ideology, then, must always be inflected by some set of local circumstances. Republicanism was not so much a unified body of dogma as a kind of language in which certain ideas could be uttered; and it was a language most frequently spoken with a regional accent.

To generalize broadly, New England had a republicanism inflected by the great Puritan myth of the City on a Hill. The two bodies of

12. Clifford Geertz, *The Interpretation of Cultures* (New York, 1973).

thought had powerful affinities with each other and consisted together well. Of course, many of the original English republicans of the seventeenth century were Puritans, which made republicanism seem a proper part of New England's intellectual heritage. And American Puritanism, like republicanism, had contradictory but interdependent historical visions. As republicanism, because of its fear of history, tended to oscillate between apocalyptic and millennial expectations, so the settlers of Massachusetts Bay moved back and forth from an exalted certainty that they were building the New Jerusalem to a black fear that their lapses of piety would cause them to falter in this mission. We are most familiar with this paradox as it was expressed in the jeremiad, New England's principal form of social criticism. Thus it was an easy matter for New Englanders, during the Revolution, to take up the republican creed, merge it with their Puritan heritage, and create a secular-millennial theory of their nation's destiny: a vision expressed by New England pamphleteers and preachers during the war and perfected in the postwar writings of poets such as Timothy Dwight and Joel Barlow. Thus too the mirror image of this millennial vision, the doom-saying conservatism of, say, the Federalist Fisher Ames.[13]

In the South republicanism was inflected by the literary myth of the pastoral. This too was a natural pairing, there being likewise strong affinities between pastoral and republican modes of thought. Just as many of the seventeenth-century English republicans had been Puritans, many of their eighteenth-century successors had argued the case for "Country" as opposed to "Court" in English politics. By associating republican virtue with the healthy pleasures of rural life, Country thinkers like Viscount Bolingbroke created a hybrid body of thought which naturally appealed to the predominantly rural South in its struggle with the North. And the pastoral also offered a historical vision which consisted well with that of republicanism. Pastoral thought, as

13. On New England republicanism, see Perry Miller, "From the Covenant to the Revival," in *Nature's Nation* (Cambridge, Mass., 1967); Sacvan Bercovitch, "How the Puritans Won the American Revolution," *Massachusetts Review*, XVII (1976), 597–630; and William C. Dowling, *Poetry and Ideology in Revolutionary Connecticut* (Athens, Ga., 1990).

Raymond Williams has argued, is built on a tension between "the plea-sures of rural settlement and the threat of loss and eviction." [14] The classic example of this tension, of course, is Virgil's first Eclogue, in which Tityrus has been deprived of his land by an edict from Rome, while Meliboeus still enjoys his as a retreat from the corruption Rome represents. As a historical vision the pastoral thus includes both the hope that the rural realm will be a secure retreat from the destructive processes of history and the fear that that realm will at last be destroyed by those processes. Like republicanism, it offers both millennial and apocalyptic visions of the future. And, like republicanism, it offers a pragmatic middle ground: the Georgic tradition, in which celebrations of pastoral peace are mingled with practical instruction on how that peace might be preserved by the arts of the good farmer. All these alternative visions of history may be seen at work in the culture of the antebellum South. All five theorists of southern identity whom I dis-cuss here were forced to pick their way among these alternatives, trying to understand the southern past and the southern future.

Pastoral republicanism was in many ways well suited to form the central theme of the southern identity. The idea was certainly well established in the region, not only among educated southerners but among others as well. As ignorant a man as Davy Crockett of Tennes-see was able, after his unlikely election to Congress, to display at least a rudimentary understanding of what a republican statesman was sup-posed to do and say. Too, republicanism lent itself naturally to the South's desire to portray itself as the true America, the section that had preserved the ideals of the Revolution; and it offered a simple account of what southerners liked to regard as the North's abandon-ment of those ideals. Such abandonments, according to republican theory, were more nearly the rule than the exception; the remarkable thing was not that some Americans had forgotten their ideals but that a few still remembered them.

Thus republican thought offered another advantage as the center-piece of a southern ideology. Because "the South" could be meaningful only in relation to "the North," theorists of southern identity needed

14. Raymond Williams, *The Country and the City* (New York, 1973), 17.

to account not just for the virtues of their own region but for the failings of its rival as well. Republicanism was by its nature dialectical, tending to divide the world between Us and Them: Country and Court, Patriot and Tory, Citizen and Tyrant, South and North. To a writer well-versed in republican theory, the moral categories would have come forth almost unbidden and arranged themselves into a neat Manichaean drama: on the one side luxury, greed, tyranny, the corrupt city; on the other virtue, independence, honor, the besieged garden. Further, this dialectical mode of thought told an apparently declining section of the country that its decline, far from being evidence of unfitness, was almost a proof of virtue. And it offered as well a comforting belief that the ideas which were undermining the South—industry, capitalism, liberal individualism, even abolition—were merely the masks of greed and interest.

Of course, republicanism encountered one great obstacle as it assumed its place as the South's dominant ideology. As it became clear in the 1830s that slavery was a permanent feature rather than a temporary blemish on the southern landscape, southerners were increasingly compelled to contemplate the conflict between their intellectual legacy and their present social order. Slavery became, in due course, the principal barrier between "ideas and substances" in southern culture. It forced Randolph and Tucker into any number of ideological contortions as they tried to maintain the republican faith in a slaveholding region. And it led Fitzhugh, who was also educated in that faith, to repudiate it at last in favor of slavery. And yet by doing so he revealed the extent to which the old faith had irrevocably shaped his thinking. Republicanism was above all a strategy for resisting tyranny, and in republican thought history was the ultimate tyrant, the force that predestined the end of republican order. For Fitzhugh and many of his southern contemporaries, history took the form of the republican heritage itself, an inheritance which, by its inescapable, silent reproach to the slaveholding region, was imposing intolerable contradictions upon it and leading it to self-destruction. Thus Fitzhugh—at the very moment when northerners like Abraham Lincoln were preparing to reject "the dogmas of the quiet past"—rejected the republican legacy and did so with a profound feeling of liberation.

Such, then, are the premises of this book. A word or two ought to be said about its scope and method. It aims, of course, to be suggestive rather than exhaustive on the creation of southern identity. I have focused on five southerners—three politicians with a bent toward literature and two fiction writers fascinated by politics—who took active and significant parts in the invention of the South. I might as easily have chosen other figures. But I have concluded that there might be a value in describing, in some detail, the long conversation about the South which was carried on over the course of fifty years by a small group of Virginians who shared nearly all their major premises. All of them inherited the republican tradition that Thomas Jefferson wielded against John Adams in the 1790s, in a struggle that became for southern republicans the heroic legend by which they defined themselves. Within the limits of chronology they knew one another, either personally or by reputation; they were neighbors, close friends, and in one case half-brothers. Over the course of two generations they pondered the history and destiny of their region, their common legacy of Virginia republicanism and its fate in the modern world, and their own roles as men of letters and public men. It was a conversation that took place while the American Union—written into existence by a Virginian with whose overwhelming legacy each man wrestled throughout his life—moved toward self-destruction. None was a "typical" southerner, whatever that might be. Nor was their Virginia a typical southern state. But they all regarded themselves as in some way representative of their region, and some of them were confirmed in this judgment by contemporaries. And although Virginia declined in wealth and power throughout the period under study, it maintained its status as the moral center of the South: a status that was ratified when the Confederacy, against all military sense, decided to seat its government in Richmond, less than a hundred miles from Washington. When these Virginians spoke for the South, that is, their words carried authority.

"Aren't you *really* an intellectual historian?" a well-known critic of southern literature asked me not long ago. His tone suggested that he had discovered a secret vice, as perhaps he had. It is no doubt apparent already, and will become more so, that I do considerable poaching in that discipline—a risky undertaking, I realize, for a literary critic. I discuss figures whose writings seem, by conventional standards, somewhat less than "literary," and one—John Randolph of Roanoke—who wrote almost nothing at all. And even when considering more conventionally literary works, one of my major concerns has been to track their social and political impetus—to account for their "cultural work," in a phrase currently popular. And so a word ought to be said in defense of this approach, which has not been the conventional one in southern literary study.

We might begin by recalling an insight of Allen Tate, who established most of the terms by which southern literature is now understood. In his essay "A Southern Mode of the Imagination," Tate cited Yeats's famous distinction—rhetoric comes from our arguments with others, poetry from our arguments with ourselves—and concluded that the highly rhetorical culture of the antebellum South produced few poets indeed. Antebellum southern writing was almost wholly lacking in irony; it was "hag-ridden" with politics; it was a literature of strident assertion rather than restless questioning. It could bear no comparison to the great literature New England was creating at the same time or to that which the South would produce a hundred years later.[15]

For Tate, of course, all of this was evidence of the Old South's cultural inferiority. In the general narrative of southern literary history which Tate developed in his several essays on the subject, this characterization of the Old South helped to clarify the superior achievement of the New, which had learned to argue with itself and thus produced a great literature. But it is possible to take Tate's insight as an invitation to consider the Old South and its literature more closely—to consider it on its own terms rather than ours.

For his argument was largely correct: the Old South was precisely a rhetorical literary culture. It could hardly have been anything else; as I began by suggesting, the region was only beginning, in the thirty years before the Civil War, to conceive and assert its existence as a separate society. Thus antebellum southern writers were, in one sense at least, working under radically different circumstances than were

15. Allen Tate, "A Southern Mode of the Imagination," in *Collected Essays* (Denver, 1959), 554–68.

their New England contemporaries who made the American Renaissance. For the New Englanders had in their defeated spiritual nation— long since impotent as a separate political realm but formidable in memory—what southern writers lacked in their emerging one: a powerful body of historical myth to respond to. The "matter of New England" became a fit subject for the meditations of historians, historical romancers, poets, even an essayist like Emerson, rather as the "matter of Scotland" had been for Sir Walter Scott. A defeated country is, of course, a romantic subject matter. But beyond that it is, like a deceased person, formidable in a way that the live thing can never be. Its unimpeachable virtues may be used to shame the living, as in Emerson's attempt to revive a version of the old Puritan piety as an alternative to the pale negations of Unitarianism. Conversely, the imagination that can confront the dead and name their failings may be energized, as Hawthorne's was, by the enormity of the undertaking: to interrogate those grim ghosts of Salem was a frightening but bracing experience. New England writers, I am saying, *had* New England, had it securely in the imagination, in a way that southern writers in the 1830s, 1840s, and 1850s, could not *have* the South. This is the difference, for example, between Hawthorne's historical fiction and that of his nearly exact contemporary, Simms. Both were regionalists, deeply learned in local history; both were historical romancers, talented students in the school of Walter Scott. But Hawthorne was able to contemplate, with a mixture of horror, awe, and sober judgment, a New England whose existence and basic identity were well established. Simms was trying, in his historical romances and his purely historical works as well, to establish such an identity for the South. Southern writers in the nineteenth century, like New Englanders in the previous two centuries, were still trying to summon their spiritual nation into existence; they could not simultaneously produce a radical critique of its constitutive myths.

Is there any point in examining the literature produced under these disadvantages? At least one recent scholar has suggested that it would be worthwhile. "We stand in our understanding of antebellum Southern thought," says the remarkable intellectual historian Michael O'Brien, "where the study of colonial New England stood when Perry

Miller came to revise the orthodoxy of Brooks Adams."[16] This statement offers not only a powerful exhortation to attend to the culture
of the Old South but also a hint of how we might best go about it. For
it directs our attention to a body of scholarship that has for generations
been anatomizing—with a thoroughness and sophistication which students of southern history can only envy—another "rhetorical" American culture. In the work of Perry Miller and the dozens of important
scholars who have followed him, we may find a model of the sort of
scholarship we might employ in recovering the culture of the Old
South. Their method was not so much a discipline as a willingness to
raid all the disciplines—with special attention to literary and historical
scholarship—in search of whatever may throw light on the culture
under study. I think that the eclecticism of this method, its casual
attitude toward disciplinary boundaries, its willingness to take a look
at nearly any sort of evidence, to take seriously nearly any sort of text,
may offer the best hope of achieving a deeper understanding of—and
maybe even a greater sympathy for—antebellum southern writing. For
example, one of the oldest clichés about the Old South is that its
literary mind was diverted into politics. If so, then the scholar who
wants to encounter that mind will need to pursue it there and to take
instruction whenever he can from other disciplines, particularly those
of political and intellectual history.

Those of us who are now inclined to take up this pursuit are fortunate to be doing so at a time when the study of southern political and
intellectual history is undergoing a remarkable renascence. Michael
O'Brien is a leading figure in this renascence; a short list of others
would include Drew Gilpin Faust, Bertram Wyatt-Brown, Kenneth
Greenberg, John McCardell, J. Mills Thornton, and many more. A
part of this movement has been fueled by particular innovations; the
explosion of scholarship on republicanism has played a part, as has the
recent attention to honor as a powerfully motivating idea in southern
life. And part of it has come simply from a willingness to take seriously

16. Michael O'Brien, *Rethinking the South: Essays in Intellectual History* (Baltimore,
1988), 20.

an intellectual culture that has usually been dismissed as limited and second-rate. But whatever its source, it offers a significant opportunity to reopen the case on antebellum southern literature and see what may be discovered.

This procedure, if we can manage it, may help us understand not only the culture of the Old South but other American cultures as well. Readers of other founding literatures in America—that of Puritan New England or of the revolutionary era—may find comparisons with the Old South instructive. Students of the New England renaissance can, by reading contemporary southerners closely, get a better sense of what is and is not unique about the literary world of Emerson and Hawthorne; they will find that northern and southern writers were equally the heirs of the old American republic and were equally concerned with comprehending and reversing antebellum America's apparent decline from republican virtue. Antebellum New Englanders and southerners all lived in a "Machiavellian moment" and often employed the same diagnostic vocabulary to make sense of it.

Students of southern literature will, of course, gain the most from a fresh look at the Old South. Though most of us will continue to care more for William Faulkner than for Nathaniel Beverley Tucker, we still ought to read the latter and his contemporaries. For if it is misleading to read the Old South in light of the New, the opposite procedure can be salutary. But in fact all students of American culture could profit in at least one way from a fresh look at the antebellum South. For most of us are now alert to the problem created by so many of the influential theories of our national literature—that such theories tend to account for only a part of American culture but to represent that part as the whole. Nina Baym has argued that such theories—with their emphasis on violent action, masculine comradeship, and the drama of the heroic self confronting nature—tend to exclude literary works by women. Russell Reising has surveyed the same general theme even more broadly, showing how large parts of the American past have proven "unusable" for the usually white, male, and northern theorists of our collective literary identity. Many Americans—women, African Americans, immigrants, and others—have been unwillingly conscripted, by the coercive "we" of the scholars, into a mythical nation that seems quite foreign to them.[17]

The South is one of the cultures which have thus been ignored (or badly misinterpreted) in order to sustain these comprehensive theories of American experience. Sacvan Bercovitch, to reach for an obvious example, relegates the South to a single footnote in his classic study *The American Jeremiad*. One may readily see why; wedded as he is to the notion of Puritan origins for the American identity, Bercovitch can see the South—the oldest part of Anglo-America and by some accounts the most typical—only as a threat to the stability of his thesis.[18] Thus he cites C. Vann Woodward as his authority for the proposition that southerners are not really quite American, then gets the title of Woodward's book wrong: *The Burden of the South*, he calls it, trying to come up with *The Burden of Southern History*. A mere slip, of course, and I am being unfair by emphasizing it, but one is powerfully tempted to regard Bercovitch's inadvertent suppression of "southern history" and his characterization of the South as a "burden" as particularly vivid representations of a very common habit among the theorists of American identity, struggling to maintain their syntheses. The South is quintessentially an insubordinate local fact, obstructing the development of any number of comprehensive accounts of the American self. Southerners, for all their failings, have been stubborn in re-

17. Nina Baym, "Melodramas of Beset Manhood: How Theories of American Fiction Exclude Women Authors," *American Quarterly*, XXXIII (1981), 123–39; Russell Reising, *The Unusable Past: Theory and the Study of American Literature* (New York, 1986).

18. Sacvan Bercovitch, *The American Jeremiad* (Madison, Wisc., 1978), xiii. The historian Jack P. Greene has recently dealt a heavy blow to the idea of America's Puritan origins. In his social history *Pursuits of Happiness: The Social Development of Early Modern British Colonies and the Formation of American Culture* (Chapel Hill, 1988), Greene argues that the dominant patterns of American life, established during the colonial years, were not those of New England but rather of the Chesapeake colonies, particularly Virginia and Maryland. Philip Gura has assessed the consequences of Greene's work for the study of American literature; see "Turning Our World Upside Down: Reconceiving Early American Literature," *American Literature*, LXIII (1991), 104–12.

sisting the idea that America must be, in Abraham Lincoln's phrase, "all one thing or all the other." A serious consideration of their culture may remind us of that and may offer as well a promising method of shaking up our certainties about our country.

I

JOHN TAYLOR AND THE IMAGE OF THE GOOD SOCIETY

In 1810 the American political situation seemed grim indeed to John Taylor of Caroline County, Virginia. It had seemed so for a long time, of course: for Taylor, as for many "Old Republicans" of the South, the country had been in decline since 1787, when the new federal Constitution supplanted the Articles of Confederation. In the years that followed they had seen the country fall further and further away from that zenith of republican virtue achieved during the Revolution. Alexander Hamilton, they believed, had tried with his "Report on Manufactures" to turn pastoral America into a manufacturing nation; and John Adams, with the Alien and Sedition Acts, had tried to turn it into a tyranny. Only the prompt action of southern republicans like himself had forestalled the threat, and only the election of Thomas Jefferson in 1800 had laid it to rest. Or so the Old Republicans had hoped, but even Jefferson turned out to be a disappointment: he soon showed himself fatally willing to compromise his republican integrity with actions like the Yazoo compromise—an attempt to override the state of Georgia's rescinding of a fraudulent land contract—and the West Florida bargain—a plan to bribe France to permit American occupation of Spanish territory in the Southwest. Such maneuvers struck Taylor as positively Federalist in their overtones of corruption and lust for power. "Federalism," he wrote to James Monroe in 1810, "indeed having been defeated, has gained a new footing, by being taken into partnership with republicanism."[1]

1. Quoted in Loren Baritz, *City on a Hill: A History of Ideas and Myths in America* (New York, 1964), 193.

The problem was severe enough to prompt many of Taylor's allies to break with Jefferson; these Tertium Quids, as the new third party was called, dedicated themselves to preserving the pure republicanism which even the president seemed willing to adulterate. Taylor, though largely retired from active politics by this time, shared the concerns of the Quids and spent these years warning whoever would listen that the nation's decline from republicanism was more than just a run of political bad luck. By 1804 he was questioning "whether mankind are capable of free, honest & moderate government, or [are] fitted only for the regimes of fraud and force." In 1806 he declared pessimistically that republicanism "contains the seeds which will cause corruption to supersede it"; and in 1807 he worried that the war which seemed to be brewing against England "may terminate in the destruction of the last experiment in favor of free government."[2] The apocalyptic tone of these warnings was not mere rhetoric; Taylor believed that Jefferson's ideological lapses constituted profound and immediate threats to the survival of the nation.

When James Madison succeeded Jefferson in the White House, the fate of the nation seemed in even greater danger. For if Jefferson had gone over to the enemy, Taylor and his friends had little doubt that Madison—an author of *The Federalist*, principal architect of the Constitution, a man widely suspected of Federalist leanings and Machiavellian principles—had pushed him. As president, Madison did very little to please the Tertium Quids, but by far his worst failing was his apparent desire for a war with England. Taylor called it a "metaphysical war," fought over an abstraction—the national honor—in the absurd confidence that the justice of the American cause would lead somehow to victory on the battlefield. America would likely lose such a war, Taylor thought, and—given the consolidated federal power that would be necessary to wage war—might lose its liberties even if it won. And so in 1810, with *de facto* Federalism back in power, with the Republican party fragmented, with the country on the brink of a disastrous war, the American situation seemed desperate. Taylor's response at first glance appears odd. He began publishing in the Quid newspaper the

2. Quoted in Shalhope, *John Taylor*, 121–23.

Spirit of '76 a series of letters, signed "Arator," on the subject of southern agricultural practice.[3]

Why did Taylor view the situation in such apocalyptic terms? And
why, viewing it thus, did he respond to the crisis by writing about the
subtle mysteries of hog-raising, and plowing, and the proper uses
of manure? What purpose were the "Arator" letters, and the book
they eventually became, meant to serve? My impression is that they
were as serious an effort as Taylor was capable of—and he was an
able man—to imagine for America a way out of its difficulties. *Arator*
is a book about farming but also about politics and economics and—
above all—about personal virtue. Most important for our purposes, it
is a book about the South—its grand potential, its disappointing reality, and its role in the destiny of America.

To see how all this may be so requires that we know a bit about John
Taylor and the way he understood the troubles his country faced in
1810. Born in 1753 to a prominent Virginia family, raised (after the
death of his parents) by a cousin, the well-known lawyer Edmund Pendleton, Taylor was descended from a long line of planter politicians.
Following the common practice for prominent Virginians of his day,
he attended the College of William and Mary, after which he was
trained in the law by Pendleton and was ready to take up a career at
the bar when the American Revolution began. During the Revolution
he served as a major in the Continental army, then as a representative
in the Virginia House of Delegates, and finally as a colonel of Virginia
militia, fighting in the Battle of Yorktown. For a decade following the
war he worked and prospered as an attorney and sometime politician.
But above all he wanted to farm, and so in 1798 he acquired Hazelwood, a plantation on the Rappahannock River, and took up life there
as a planter.

3. Shalhope points out that Taylor increased his literary productivity generally in
response to the crises of the moment, even accelerating the laconic pace of his work
on his magnum opus, *An Inquiry into the Principles and Policy of the Government of the
United States*, in progress for almost twenty years. But it was to *Arator* that he gave
most of his energy.

When Taylor bought it, Hazelwood was a run-down, depleted, and unproductive farm, having been nearly ruined by a dissolute young aristocrat of the Shirley family. Taylor set about reforming it, undertaking agricultural experiments designed to discover the most effective means of regenerating depleted soil. These experiments were the genesis of the agricultural instruction in *Arator.* He became a widely recognized expert in scientific agriculture: his successes at reforming his land were the stuff of local legend, and Hazelwood came to be regarded as a model Virginia farm, to which other planters often came to learn the arts of agriculture. Taylor eventually won the presidency of the Virginia Agricultural Society, an office he preferred, he said, to the presidency of the United States.

He certainly preferred it to all lesser offices, for though he was bred to political power and served several times in the Virginia Assembly and the U.S. Senate, Taylor showed all his life a positive distaste for elective politics. When he held an office it was usually because he had been called to it unwillingly, and he usually quit at the first opportunity, invariably explaining his departure by comparing the corruption of politics to the virtuous rural life of his farm. "Hereafter," he wrote Jefferson on leaving the Virginia Assembly in 1799, "I mean to till a soil which promises to crown my labor with some success. . . . It was foolish of me to leave the bosom which nourished me for the sake of exposing my own to the unfraternal shafts of all the wicked passions." [4] As Thomas Hart Benton observed of him after his death, Taylor's political career consisted of "giving his time to his farm and his books, when not called by emergency to the public service—and returning to his books and farm when the emergency was over." [5] He spent his days writing about republicanism and agriculture, the two subjects concerning which, as he confessed to Jefferson, "there is a spice of fanaticism in my nature." [6]

4. Henry H. Simms, *Life of John Taylor: The Story of a Brilliant Leader in the Early Virginia State Rights School* (Richmond, 1932), 155.

5. Thomas Hart Benton, *Thirty Years' View: A History of the Working of the American Government for Thirty Years, from 1820 to 1850* (New York, 1854), 45.

6. Baritz, *City on a Hill*, 163.

Taylor's thinking on these subjects was complex, largely because it was unsystematic: he was almost entirely an *a posteriori* thinker who thoroughly distrusted intellectual systems. He tried once to hammer his political thought into an orderly pattern, in his massive *Inquiry into the Principles and Policy of the Government of the United States* (1814), a work twenty years in the making; the finished product was a book marked by considerable insight but nearly impenetrable logic and prose. "For heaven's sake," said his friend John Randolph when the *Inquiry* appeared, "get some worthy person to do the second edition into *English*." [7] Since then several scholars have, with varying degrees of success, made similar efforts to draw up blueprints of Taylor's thought. It may be that the effort is in some degree misguided, that his worldview cannot without distortion be systematized; my own impression is that he came nearest to explaining himself in his haphazard, occasionally poetic but never systematic farming manual, *Arator*. But for our purposes Taylor's thought can be understood adequately in a series of related dichotomies with which he tried to understand most of the issues of his day.

The first of these opposed the farm, symbolizing virtue, to the urban world of commerce, politics, and corruption. This opposition was illustrated by the pattern we have already noticed in Taylor's public career—his tendency to accept political office reluctantly and to resign from it eagerly, always to return to farming. Hazelwood was the natural home of virtue, "the bosom which nourished me"; Washington and Richmond were dens of corruption, full of "all the wicked passions." This dichotomy was informed in part, of course, by the ancient poetic tradition of the pastoral, with its association of rural life with virtue, simplicity, order, and wholeness—associations as old as Theocritus but particularly powerful, as Leo Marx has shown, in America, where for some the pastoral was no mere poetic convention but a living reality. Taylor lived at a time when this reality was giving way, when (to cite Marx's findings again) the pastoral ideal in America was becoming again a mere poetic symbol, a "momentary stay against confusion."

---

7. Quoted in Norman K. Risjord, *The Old Republicans: Southern Conservatism in the Age of Jefferson* (New York, 1965), 150.

Even Jefferson would soon admit the need to make room for the machine in the American garden.[8] Taylor never conceded so much; for him the American pastoral vision expressed a viable economic and social system, a real and permanent refuge from the corrupt world of getting and spending.

Taylor's stubbornness on this point was owing, perhaps, to the other main source of his agrarianism, which was not poetic but political. He was (like many Americans of the revolutionary generation, as several recent historians have shown) an heir of the Country tradition of English politics, an eighteenth-century British version of Greek, Roman, and Venetian "classical republicanism." The thought of Country philosophers like Viscount Bolingbroke turned on a single theme: the idea of an ongoing struggle, endemic to political life, between governmental power and the virtuous independence of the citizen. Government always tried to expand itself, mainly by transforming citizens into its economic dependents. Hence the civic virtue of the citizen—his capacity for disinterested political judgment—depended on his being economically independent and thus immune to the financial blandishments offered by the self-aggrandizing state. The most reliable source of such independence, for many republican thinkers, was land: farmers were in any republic the principal repositories of civic virtue. To concede the end of the pastoral was, for an heir of the Country tradition, almost to concede the end of republican order. It was a concession Taylor was never willing to make.

To say this is to bring up the next of Taylor's organizing dichotomies: a dichotomy, roughly speaking, between republicanism and history. Like most American politicians of his day, Taylor believed that republican government was by its nature fragile and short-lived, that over time it was likely to degenerate into anarchy or tyranny. History—the realm of time and change—was itself an enemy of republican order.[9]

8. Leo Marx, *The Machine in the Garden: Technology and the Pastoral Ideal in America* (New York, 1964); see Jefferson's letter to Benjamin Austin, January 9, 1816, in Jefferson, *Writings,* ed. Merrill Peterson (New York, 1984), 1369–72.

9. As Pocock shows throughout *The Machiavellian Moment,* republican order was usually taken to represent a balance of some sort: between land and capital, local and federal power, country and city, and so on. Thus change was by definition a threat to the republic: in an equilibrium any change is change for the worse.

This idea America also learned from the English Country thinkers, who had taught that even in a republic of virtuous landholders the government would eventually succeed at corrupting many of the citizens. Thus the state tended inevitably toward moral decline, a decline which could be reversed only by a difficult return to the first principles of the commonwealth. The Country view, that is, involved a keen awareness of contemporary vice coupled with a certainty that times had once been better and could, by restorative effort, be made so again. This combination made for a distinctly nonprogressive view of history: at worst, the life of a republic was a simple pattern of decline; at best, it might be a cycle, an endless round of decay and regeneration.

This fear of republican mortality was the context of Taylor's many apocalyptic warnings about the imminent end of republican order in America, and he was, of course, far from being the only American to utter such warnings. This fear was a major preoccupation of American politics in the Early National period: how could America preserve itself from the usual fate of republican government? The framers of the Constitution had already offered their answer: shrewdly constructed governmental forms designed to mitigate the self-destructive tendencies of republicanism. Others, including many of the Antifederalists, insisted that what mattered was not the organization of the government but the virtue of the citizens: as long as that virtue lasted, the republic would endure. How might it be sustained? One way was somehow to preserve the spirit of that moment of supreme national virtue, the Revolution—thus the assertion, quite common in the political speech of the Early National period, that the Revolution was in some sense unfinished, that all the travails of the young nation, and even other nationalist movements around the world, must be regarded as continuations of the struggle. One recalls that President James Monroe would for ceremonial occasions don the revolutionary uniform he had worn as a twenty-year-old lieutenant, as if, George Forgie comments, "to ward off not the British, but time itself." The idea was to prolong, Grecian urn–like, what was by its nature a transitory moment of passion. For a great many others, a better answer lay in the unexplored West: if political virtue depended in part on landed independence, then what Henry Nash Smith has called the "fee-simple empire" offered a way of delaying the eventual republican day of reckoning so long as the land held out. Both of these impulses were at work among the war hawks of 1810; the war that actually broke out two years later was often called "the second American Revolution," and among its announced ends was the acquisition of additional North American land. Such efforts to stave off history, or to escape it by lighting out for the territory, all aimed to seal America off from time's usual and perhaps inevitable way with republican government.[10]

Although Taylor shared the fears of these Americans, he distrusted most of the solutions they proposed. He did not believe, as did the constitutional framers, that the answer lay in shrewdly constructed governmental forms: "to contend for forms only," he said, "is to fight for shadows."[11] There was no system of government so well designed as to be proof against tyranny and none so bad that it could not, in the right hands, yield good results. Accordingly, he placed most of his emphasis on the question of civic virtue. But he distrusted efforts to preserve that virtue by shielding it from the processes of history. He considered it dangerous to perpetuate the revolutionary spirit by a policy of belligerence toward England. "The habit of blowing up a mob," he warned, "as boys blow up bladders, which by heating are made to burst with a great noise, is a dangerous tampering with our government at its base."[12] Taylor wanted sober, reliable citizens, not chronically agitated jingoists. The solution offered by the frontier was no better. The constantly migrating nomad required by the westward movement was just the opposite of Taylor's ideal American, settled on his acres; and the idea of a "fee-simple empire," with the energetic federal power needed to seize and maintain it, directly contradicted his preference for a small, stable, unaggressive republic, governed minimally and locally. Most of the suggested cures for republican malaise seemed, to Taylor, as bad as the disease. They implied an America in a perpetual

10. George B. Forgie, *Patricide in the House Divided: A Psychological Interpretation of Lincoln and His Age* (New York, 1979), 49; Henry Nash Smith, *Virgin Land: The American West as Symbol and Myth* (Cambridge, Mass., 1950).

11. John Taylor, *Construction Construed and Constitutions Vindicated* (Richmond, 1820), 13.

12. Quoted in Shalhope, *John Taylor*, 126.

state of nervous excitement and peripatetic activity, frantically trying to outrun history; they proposed that reflexive, goalless progressivism which a later southern agrarian, John Crowe Ransom, identified as "pioneering on principle." Taylor was both temperamentally and ideologically uncomfortable with such pioneering; he would have agreed with Ransom's judgment that "the pioneering life is not the normal life, whatever some Americans may suppose."[13]

But with pioneering on principle ruled out, what remedy was there for the apparently inevitable mortality of republican order? Where, to borrow another phrase from the later agrarians, was republicanism to "take its stand"? Taylor answered the question in his book about the southern farm, which brings up the last of the organizing dichotomies in Taylor's thought and the one that draws our attention to him in the first place: the sectional opposition, North and South. For Taylor republicanism and the pastoral converged in the South, which made him one of the earliest sectionalists in American politics. "To penetrate his thought," Robert Shalhope writes, "is to witness the transformation of Revolutionary republicanism, once held in common with the larger national community, into a sectional ideology." As early as the revolutionary war, when most Americans were still enjoying the novelty of Union, Taylor's more sensitive seismograph was already detecting tremors of sectional conflict. From the battlefield he reported to his kinsman Philip Pendleton that the soldiers of the North were really "mercenaries" and that those of the West were wild and undisciplined: the fate of America depended, he thought, on the yeoman volunteers of the South. Later in the war, while serving in the Virginia House of Delegates, Taylor drafted a stern protest against what seemed to him a cooling in New England's enthusiasm for the struggle, now that the battlefront had moved south. During the fight over constitutional ratification Taylor was a staunch Antifederalist, apparently because, like many of his Virginia colleagues, he identified the more centralized constitutional government with commerce, thus with the North. Cer-

13. John Crowe Ransom, "Reconstructed but Unregenerate," in Twelve Southerners, *I'll Take My Stand: The South and the Agrarian Tradition* (New York, 1930), 4.

tainly ever afterward he tended to regard commerce, federal power, and the North as an almost inseparable unholy triptych.[14]

Taylor's system of political geography owed much to mere local patriotism, but it also reflected his serious efforts to comprehend the perplexities of the new American Union within his vocabulary of Anglo-American republicanism. That body of thought, organized around the idea of virtue's losing battle with corruption, almost necessarily encouraged the disposition to see evidence of decline everywhere and then to look for scapegoats on whom to blame it. If the country had once been virtuous, and now was not, then something must have corrupted it. Bernard Bailyn has described the nearly automatic response of American colonists, steeped in English republican thought, to the new assertion of British colonial power after 1763: their political tradition gave them no choice but to interpret the change as a conspiracy against their liberties by an insatiably expansive government.[15] It appears that something similar took place in Taylor's mind when he began to detect signs of sectional conflict in the new Union. In a country governed by a radically flawed Constitution, ruled by a *de facto* Federalist, and spoiling for an imperialist war with Britain, Taylor had no trouble concluding that something had gone wrong. Given his southern and agrarian loyalties, it is hardly surprising that he looked north for the source of the trouble. The country's hope, now as in the Revolution, lay in the agrarian, liberty-loving South, the last preserve of republican and pastoral virtue.

14. Shalhope, *John Taylor,* 9, 23, 50. Shalhope also cites a more personal example of Taylor's view of the relation between North and South (and of the view—identical but with poles reversed—held by a representative Yankee republican): Taylor's 1805 epistolary exchange with Timothy Dwight, the president of Yale. Dwight had charged the southern students at New Haven with habitual sloth and love of luxury and hinted that these traits were characteristic of their region. Far from it, Taylor retorted; in fact those traits—which both men recognized as antithetical to republican virtue—belonged mainly to the rich merchants of New England. A "Boston nabob," said Taylor, might spend as much on an evening's entertainment as a hardworking Virginia farmer made in a year (*ibid.,* 113).

15. Bailyn, *Ideological Origins.*

Such were the ideas by which Taylor assessed his country's troubles in 1810. It remains to be seen just how he put them to work in his remarkable personal statement, *Arator*. One is not surprised to notice that the work is more than a farming manual: for Taylor agriculture was related to a host of political, economic, and moral issues, and his book addresses them as well. "Ostensibly written to encourage agricultural reforms," Shalhope explains, "the 'Arator' essays actually presented an ideal view of society, until then only barely discernible in Taylor's work." He does not present this view literally, of course; it is hard to imagine so intensely practical a man as Taylor writing a utopian tract. Instead he chose to suggest the outlines of an ideal society by portraying in loving detail that society's representative institution, the well-managed farm. There were, he believed, important metaphoric correspondences between pastoral life and republican governance: in both, as Taylor says in the preface to *Arator*, "renewal must constantly follow close upon the heels of decay, either to maintain fertility or to avoid oppression." [16] Unlike many of the actual Virginia farms Taylor knew, his ideal farm (modeled, of course, on his own Hazelwood) was to exist in harmony with nature. Rather than exhaust the soil by planting, the good farmer of Taylor's description enriches it; after all, as the author explains, "arts improve the work of nature—when they injure it, they are not arts, but barbarous customs" (69). Because he replenishes rather than depletes his soil by planting, this farmer is not made to become a nomad, constantly wandering westward in search of new fields to plant; he may remain where he is, sink roots in the community around him, and become the sort of stable, reliable citizen on whom Taylor thought the fortunes of the republic depended. Existing thus in harmony with nature, this farmer achieved not just economic self-sufficiency and social stability but personal virtue as well. "Poetry," he says in a late chapter, "in allowing more virtue to agriculture, than to any other profession, has abandoned her privilege of fiction, and yielded to the natural moral effect of the absence of temptation" (315).

Anyone will, of course, recognize this ideal southern farm and its

16. Shalhope, *John Taylor*, 127; Taylor, *Arator*, 57, hereafter cited in the text by page number.

proprietor as the stock figures of pastoral poetry from Virgil's *Eclogues* onward. Like nearly everything in this genre, *Arator* offers the rural landscape as an image of wholeness and purity to be contrasted, at least by implication, with the fragmentation and corruption of the city. It was not the first time the South had been employed in this symbolic capacity: one thinks of Michael Drayton's "To the Virginian Voyage" (1606), which identified the new colony as "Earth's only paradise," where the fruits of nature could be had almost without labor; or of the pamphlets of the Virginia Company, which offered it as a place where cherished rural institutions, endangered by demographic changes in England, could flourish again; or of William Byrd's well-known letter to Lord Orrery (1726), in which he concluded a somewhat defensive description of Virginia life by insisting that "we are very happy in our Canaans if we could but forget the Onions and Fleshpots of Egypt."[17] The Virgilian pastoral tradition in which *Arator* participates may be the oldest and most powerful one in southern writing.

Following that tradition—in which, as Raymond Williams points out, "the contrast . . . is between the pleasures of rural settlement and the threat of loss and eviction"—Taylor hardly begins his celebration of the virtuous Virginia farm before telling us that it is about to be destroyed.[18] Citing the findings of William Strickland, a recent English observer, Taylor asserts that American and particularly southern farms now produce less, that farmers are poorer, and that the land itself is less fertile than ever before. Planters were ruining their lands, as Hazelwood itself had been ruined, and then abandoning them in favor of new ones to the west. What had caused all this trouble? "If agriculture is bad and languishing in a country and climate, where it may be good and prosperous," Taylor says, "no doubt remains with me, that political institutions have chiefly perpetrated the evil" (73). Northern specu-

17. Michael Drayton, "To the Virginian Voyage," in *The Golden Hind: An Anthology of Elizabethan Prose and Poetry*, ed. Roy Lamson and Hallett Smith (New York, 1942), 417; William Byrd, "Letter to Lord Orrery," in *Southern Writing, 1585–1920*, ed. Richard Beale Davis, C. Hugh Holman, and Louis D. Rubin, Jr. (New York, 1970), 111–13. On the pamphlets of the Virginia Company, see Richard Gray, *Writing the South: Ideas of an American Region* (Cambridge, Eng., 1986), 1–10.

18. Williams, *The Country and the City*, 17.

lators, he charges, have come to dominate the central government and are using its tariffs effectively to steal the honest earnings of farmers. The hard-pressed farmers, attempting to force larger and more lucrative crops from their lands, are thus systematically ruining them. Taylor spends the first twelve chapters of his book elaborating upon this theme and thus depicting the classic situation of the Virgilian pastoral: as in the *Eclogues* (and in such roughly contemporaneous English pastorals as Oliver Goldsmith's *Deserted Village*), the virtuous rural world is here threatened by the corrupt city, by political power in the service of commerce.

Certainly Taylor's evocation of the Virgilian tradition in a portrait of the well-run farm and its proprietor was in one sense an appropriate answer to the problems his America faced in 1810. The good farmer, settled on his land and in his community, was metaphorically a good reproach to the opposing ideal of the American as physical or spiritual wanderer, devoted only to the ideal of progress, to pioneering on principle. But what practical good did it do to paint such a portrait, particularly given that, as Taylor makes plain, it is the portrait of institutions that are vanishing? One possible answer, partially valid, is that *Arator* is what Leo Marx calls a "complex" pastoral, one which portrays an idealized rural landscape in order to call it into question, to "bring irony to bear against the illusion of peace and harmony in a green pasture."[19] In many of the complex pastorals which Marx discusses, the only peace finally available is that afforded by the literary work itself; the only secure retreat from the corrupt world is the retreat into imagination. Is Taylor's good farm then a mere metaphor, offered in quixotic, nostalgic protest against the irresistible tendencies of the age? Is *Arator* a book like, say, *Walden*, a purely literary gesture of resistance to the encroaching materialism of the modern age?

In a way it is. Certainly Taylor idealizes life in nature, and certainly he anticipates Henry Thoreau's dismay at a world in which so many were condemned, by alleged progress, to lives of quiet desperation. He wrote *Arator*, he says, in the hope that "a system which sheds happiness, plenty and virtue all around, will gradually be substituted for one,

19. Marx, *Machine in the Garden*, 25.

which fosters vice, breeds want, and begets misery" (316)—he wrote it, as he might have said if he had had Thoreau's ear for prose, to wake his neighbors up. But *Arator* differs sharply from *Walden* in at least one significant way, and the difference may help clarify what sort of pastoral Taylor's book is. For if Taylor was no artist and hardly the stylist Thoreau was, it seems fair to point out that Thoreau was not the farmer Taylor was. *Walden's* discussion of "economy" is after all more or less of a joke: the author's bean-raising experiment lost money, and the profits of his retreat were, he makes it plain, to be looked for elsewhere than the ledger book—and ultimately, elsewhere than the shores of Walden Pond. One suspects that Taylor would have been mystified by this idea. He would have recognized those other profits, of course, but they would have struck him as ephemeral so long as the books failed to balance: a man raising beans at a loss, on borrowed land, would for him have achieved only a very tenuous sort of redemption. Taylor is utterly serious about the process of social and moral regeneration, but he is quite as serious about hogs and manure and enclosures and quite certain that these two categories of value depend absolutely on each other. Chief for him among "the pleasures of agriculture," as he declares in the chapter of that title, was that of "fitting ideas to substances and substances to ideas" (313): the ideas alone were not enough. If Thoreau's vision is transcendental, then Taylor's is incarnational. He distrusts abstractions and is willing to credit metaphysical concepts only if they are, so to speak, made flesh. He was not the man to be contented with a momentary stay against confusion, a merely imaginative escape from the destructive modern age.

Actually Taylor's work participates not only in the "Arcadian" pastoral tradition of the *Eclogues* but also, as M. E. Bradford has argued, in that of "hard pastoral": like Virgil's *Georgics* and Cato's *De Agricultura*, it mixes its moral instruction with "practical agricultural advice."[20] Indeed, the great bulk of *Arator* consists not of idealizations of rural life or lamentations for its passing but precisely of such advice, presented in sometimes mind-numbing detail. Taylor does not merely

---

20. M. E. Bradford, "A Virginia Cato: John Taylor of Caroline and the Agrarian Republic," Introduction to Taylor, *Arator*, 37.

sketch out the good farm as a convenient metaphor for the good life; he explains exactly how that farm must be run: where to put the barn, what to feed the hogs, what sort of clover to use in the fourth shift of the planting cycle. "Details," he explains early on, in the spirit of fair warning, "however unentertaining, may not be useless; therefore I shall often resort to them" (146). Indeed he does, to such an extent that anyone who has made his way through *Arator*'s eight consecutive chapters entitled "Manuring," or its six called "Draining," or its four on "Indian corn," anyone who has pondered its comparative analysis of "culmiferous," "succulent," and "leguminous" crops, will likely dissent from Shalhope's judgment that the book is only "ostensibly" about agriculture. One suspects that for Taylor its value as an image of wholeness offered to an America on the brink of disintegration was precisely in its dual nature. The good farm portrayed in *Arator* is a symbolic representation of a virtuous republic, but it is also simply a good farm, the practical foundation of that republic. The farm is a metaphor, and something more besides.

Just what more it is we can discover by considering Taylor's departures from the Virgilian pastoral formula. The most notable such departure may be his curious unwillingness in *Arator* to preserve the conventional moral contrast between country and city, pastoral South and commercial North. He spends the first twelve chapters of his book establishing that contrast, but he spends most of the remainder complicating it. Having described the city's threat to the southern garden, he then directs our attention to the garden itself, and there brings us up short. "Slavery" is the title of the thirteenth chapter; Taylor virtually slaps his readers in the face with what he considered the gravest moral problem confronting pastoral republicanism in the South and spends considerable time discussing the depth and difficulty of the problem. It is hardly what one would expect in either a pastoral idyll or a polemical defense of southern society. And he continues in this vein for the next two hundred pages, discussing not just slavery but a host of southern economic and social problems, tirelessly adding count after count to his indictment of the region for sloth, stupidity, and injustice. This second part of the book seems almost a complete contradiction of the first: here the garden itself is corrupt, never mind what may threaten it from outside. *Et in Arcadia ego* might be the epigraph. Why does Taylor implicate his pastoral world in the corruptions of the modern age, thus blurring the simple moral contours of his book? We can best answer the question, perhaps, by pausing to consider in detail Taylor's discussion of slavery, letting his treatment of this direst flaw in southern society illustrate his usual method in confronting such problems. For this treatment reveals a great deal not just about Taylor himself but about pastoral republican ideology as a means of apprehending southern realities, some of which it revealed in sharp detail and some of which it obscured completely.

Taylor could not have hoped to emerge from this discussion with any comforting news about the problem of slavery or any simple solutions to it. His own thinking about the issue, after all, was based on his commitment to a pair of conflicting imperatives. On one hand he was a republican, one of those "men of Jeffersonian conscience" than whom, says Richard Brown, "no men in America were more honestly committed to the notion that [slavery] was wrong."[21] He would not, like later southern political thinkers, defend slavery as a "positive good" which served the interests of slaves as well as masters. But on the other hand, Taylor feared that emancipation, unless it were managed properly, would lead (as it had recently in Santo Domingo) to racial warfare. Thus he could not, like the French republicans of that island, advocate immediate and general emancipation without thought to what would follow. "Were the whites of St. Domingo," he asked, "morally bound to bring on themselves that massacre produced by the liberation of their slaves? Is such a sacrifice of freemen, to make freemen of slaves, virtuous or wicked?" (176–77).

When he thought about slavery, that is, Taylor faced an impasse. How perplexing he found it, and how determined he was to find a way through, may be inferred from his discussion of it in *Arator*: he devotes two early chapters to the subject, and then—apparently dissatisfied—returns to it in a late chapter and in a note. The solutions he eventually arrived at seem characteristic of Taylor's mingled idealism and practi-

21. Quoted in Anne Norton, *Alternative Americas: A Reading of Antebellum Political Culture* (Chicago, 1986), 114.

cality, not to mention his willingness to plunge undaunted into end-lessly vexed questions.

In *Arator* Taylor begins his discussion of these questions by taking issue with Jefferson's similar discussion in *Notes on the State of Virginia*. The way he does so is revealing. On the facts of the case he largely agrees with Jefferson: slavery is a moral evil and a contradiction of republicanism, a problem the South must solve as quickly and pru-dently as possible. What troubles him is the dire tone of Jefferson's warnings, the insistence that slavery would undermine the republican spirit of the South and the implication that the problem would likely be resolved by an apocalyptic confrontation between slaves and mas-ters, with God himself taking the side of the oppressed. Jefferson, of course, had written in 1787, before the Santo Domingo uprising of 1791; he had been able in "Query 18" of the *Notes* to contemplate a racial apocalypse—"Indeed I tremble for my country when I reflect that God is just, that his justice cannot sleep forever"—and then im-mediately, in "Query 19," to imagine a kind of pastoral millennium, involving neither slaves nor masters but only "those who labor in the earth," the chosen people of God.[22] To Taylor, writing after Santo Do-mingo, the apocalypse may have seemed too real and the millennial vision, following so suddenly on its heels, too sanguine. In any case, his own discussion of the problem seems intended as a dose of cold water poured over the heated issue: he is determined to adopt the language of calm common sense.

Thus he tries to thread a course between Jefferson's extremes, be-tween apocalypse and millennium, and so discover the means whereby his society can solve the moral problem of slavery without being de-stroyed in the process. "The fact is," he says, "that Negro slavery is an evil which the United States must look in the face. To whine over it, is cowardly; to aggravate it, criminal; to forbear to alleviate it, because it cannot be wholly cured, foolish" (180). Accordingly, in *Arator* he outlines plans for the immediate "alleviation" of the evil as well as for its eventual elimination. He suggests a plan to give the free blacks of the South, who normally lived in terrible destitution, arable lands to

22. Jefferson, *Notes on the State of Virginia*, in *Writings*, 289–90.

cultivate in the western territories and the means to move there (118); and he proposes—uncharacteristically for this enemy of governmental power—that strict new laws be created to protect slaves from mistreatment (357).

As for the long-term solution to the problem, Taylor concluded, like many other southerners (and some northerners, including the young William Lloyd Garrison), that slaves must be liberated gradually and then somehow relocated outside the South. But how was this to be done? The question had been taken up by another recent writer on the subject, the Virginia lawyer and poet St. George Tucker, in his widely read *Dissertation on Slavery* (1796). Tucker had demonstrated mathematically that the transportation of the southern slave population to Africa would be an undertaking of enormous—he thought prohibitive—expense. Thus he had recommended that slaves be gradually liberated, to satisfy the claims of conscience, and then left to shift for themselves in the South. Acknowledging that this dispossessed class would be a continuing problem for the region, he recommended that the freedmen be deprived of all political and most civil rights, on the frankly heartless ground that such injustice would soon induce them to move at their own expense to some place more inviting. The South would thus rid itself of a sticky problem, and do so at a bargain price as well.

The logical neatness of Tucker's demonstrations gave his book a wide and enthusiastic following in the South. Taylor does not mention *A Dissertation on Slavery* in *Arator,* though he was almost certainly familiar with it. But he does reject its central idea: he insists that the transportation of freed slaves to some place where their "virtue, religion, and liberty" may be "reanimated" (125) must be undertaken at public expense. What he must have thought of Tucker's plan to drive the freedmen out by a program of calculated injustice may be inferred from his discussion of the condition of the free blacks already living in the South. He saw clearly the plight of a people who contended constantly against racial prejudice and did so, as Taylor says, aided by neither the rights of the free citizen nor even the relative security of the slave. Lacking other means of subsistence, they were often reduced to thievery. He would have considered it both unjust and enormously imprudent to thrust such conditions on the whole black population of the South. The only solution was that slaves must be emancipated, one at a time if necessary, and transported at public or charitable expense to some place where they could cultivate virtue and liberty and live the only sorts of lives Taylor thought worth living.

Thus Taylor leads his readers through a painstaking consideration of possible responses to the evil of slavery, from the destructive idealism of republican France to the cold-blooded practicality of a St. George Tucker, and arrives at last at what he considered the only genuine solution to the problem. The resulting meditation is typical of Taylor. One detects in it little systematic racism. Taylor attributes any moral deficiencies in southern slaves to slavery itself, not to intrinsic racial flaws, and he has no doubt that African Americans, like other Americans, will cultivate "virtue, religion and liberty" when given a chance. And he at least occasionally pauses to mention the glaring point so often overlooked by southern antislavery writers: that slavery injured not only masters but the slaves themselves. Though his tone is relentlessly practical and far from sentimental, Taylor displays an empathy for the victims of the institution which might surprise us.

Yet Taylor's sympathy for slaves is decisively curbed by his fear of revolt: he insists, no doubt with Santo Domingo in mind, that slaves be strictly controlled until the moment of their emancipation. And he seems never even to have considered the possibility that freed slaves might cultivate tobacco, along with virtue, religion, and liberty, alongside their former masters in the South. Thus his unquestioned assumption, shared with most of his contemporaries who addressed the same question, that any plan of emancipation must rest upon the almost inconceivably vast project of transporting the entire southern black population elsewhere—to Africa or the western territories.

This last point seems most telling because it seems to have involved Taylor in uncomfortable contradictions. His recommendation of the virtually impossible project of transportation seems at odds with his habitual practicality. And his blithe willingness to uproot a well-established population—some black families, after all, had been in Virginia longer than his own—strongly contradicts his usual preference for rootedness and his contempt for nomadic mobility. His inability even to imagine what now seems the obvious alternative to transportation—to include the freed slaves in the southern community, trusting pastoral and republican institutions to make virtuous citizens of them—is revealing. To be sure, it rests in part on his hardheaded recognition of the "incurable prejudices" of his neighbors, who would make life difficult for such freedmen as remained in Virginia (120). But even more important, it rests on his assumption, which comes directly from the republican creed, that successful republics require homogeneous populations: that the citizens of a republic must be at one in opinions, interests, and—implicitly—race. A multiracial republic was by its nature doomed; even if it avoided racial violence, it was sure to fall victim to the great political evil of "faction." In the end Taylor found it easier to imagine the whole southern black population marching westward (or embarking for Africa)—and easier to stomach the coercive injustice of this forced removal—than to imagine a racially mixed republic. I began by suggesting that republicanism was a language in which certain ideas could be uttered; it was also, as Taylor's struggle with the slavery issue reveals, a language in which some ideas could not even be conceived.

Taylor's solution to the problem of slavery may now seem wildly impractical, but he pursued it, as was his wont, with hardheaded determination. In *Arator* he insists that his countrymen look the evil of slavery in the face and take responsible action. And in 1816, six years after writing his farming manual, he became a founder and principal benefactor of the American Colonization Society, formed to put his difficult solution into effect. The man who had brought Hazelwood back from ruin—whatever his other failings—was not accustomed to turn away from difficulties.

Taylor's discussion of slavery is typical of his treatment of the internal problems of the South: throughout he refuses to idealize his society, to minimize its difficulties, or to blame outsiders for the problems southerners had brought on themselves. Why does he do it? Taylor seems to have conceived his pastoral world less as a refuge from the destructive forces of history than as an advantageous place to confront them. He hopes to describe a pastoral scene that is not ephemeral, not doomed by the evils of commerce, or slavery, or incompetent farming—and thus to suggest a republican order that is likewise more durable than such orders were generally taken to be, one that can confront its problems and survive them, can turn and face history rather than run perpetually away from it.

The relentlessly practical tone of *Arator* is interrupted only once, in the late chapter to which I have already referred, "The Pleasures of Agriculture." This essay, remarkable as one of Taylor's few attempts at lyricism, is in a sense the thematic heart of his book. Having through fifty-eight chapters tirelessly and dutifully addressed all the political and agricultural woes of his country and region, Taylor here gives his emotions free rein in what he terms a "eulogy" for the farming life. The farmer, he explains, is a greater patriot than even the military hero, as may be seen "by a comparison between a system of agriculture which doubles the fertility of a country, and a successful war which doubles its territory"—the former gain enriching the country, the latter costing it blood and treasure (315). Just as Jefferson had said, the farmer is favored by God himself, the "divine intelligence" having after all "selected an agricultural state as a paradise for its first favorites"; and the farmers of our age, who daily follow the divine injunction to feed the hungry and clothe the naked, are assured of admission to heaven (314). As for the pleasures of the farming life, Taylor asserts, in an obviously heartfelt passage, that they are considerable: "The novelty, frequency and exactness of accommodations between our ideas and operations, constitutes the most exquisite source of mental pleasure. Agriculture feeds it with endless supplies in the natures of soils, plants, climates, manures, instruments of culture and domestic animals. Their combinations are inexhaustible, discrimination and adaption are never idle, and unsatiated interest receives gratification in quick succession" (313–14). "In short," he concludes, by exercising body and mind, by combining experience of the practical world with knowledge of "the arcana of nature," and by habituation to the practice of morality, agriculture serves as "the best architect of a complete man" (316).

Taylor manages his "eulogy" clumsily enough, of course, as the passages I have quoted make painfully clear: the disparity between the depth of his feeling and the prose that must carry it is almost heartbreaking. And yet for all its awkwardness, "The Pleasures of Agriculture" does manage a poetic intensity that makes it stand out sharply from the rest of *Arator*. It is in a way surprising that the book does not end here, with an outburst of sentiment which to anyone else might have seemed the ideal conclusion for this celebration of the southern pastoral realm. But Taylor, deaf or indifferent to the claims of literary symmetry, clears his throat and presses on, concluding his book with a remarkable decrescendo: "The Rights of Agriculture," "Agriculture and the Militia," "Cotton," "Hay and Fodder," and "The Present and Political State of Agriculture." Perhaps this anticlimax is simply more evidence of Taylor's literary tin ear. But if so it is one of several moments when his very awkwardness acquires charm, even power. It works, to begin with, as a kind of *bona fides:* one has the feeling that only an honest man would write so artlessly. But beyond this there is an appropriateness in the dying fall with which *Arator* concludes. The teaching of the book, were it distilled in a single statement, might be that truth inheres in small details as much as in big ideas: in poetic notions about the pleasures of agriculture but also in the daily routine of farm life; in books but also in experience; in Washington, perhaps, but also in Caroline County and all the communities like it, where the real life of the country is lived and where its virtue must be preserved. This truth is not final but provisional, the product of experience and thus subject to the revisions of further experience; it is not millennial but resolutely historical, able to take its chances in the realm of time and change. Thus the appropriateness of Taylor's refusal to end his book with a kind of beatific vision: his republican farmer may, after his fashion, achieve such a vision, but afterward he returns to the world, ready to fight the next battle. An awareness of "the pleasures of agriculture" does not relieve him of the daily obligation to think about hay and fodder and the fortunes of republican government.

Arator, then, makes the case for a realistic confrontation of the problems facing an agrarian republic. But it does more than that; considered formally, what the book accomplishes, by juxtaposing unsparing dissections of the South's social ills with panegyrics to the pleasures of agriculture, is to *represent* the necessity of such confrontation. We see the farm, which symbolizes order and wholeness, but we cannot escape seeing, right next to it, various embodiments of history: slavery and tariffs, corrupt politicians and lazy farmers. The effect is like the one Edmund Spenser achieves in *The Faerie Queene* by placing the figure of Time in the idyllic Garden of Adonis: the image communicates that the pastoral realm and the order it represents inevitably exist in history, not in spite of it. This was a profound teaching in an America given to pioneering on principle. The vision of order embodied in the pastoral republic, Taylor was saying, must be able to withstand the pressures of history, not merely escape them, imaginatively or in (temporary) reality. *Arator* provides not just an image of virtue but also a description of the daily practical labor by which virtue, in the real world, must be maintained. It is in this sense that a book which never wandered very far from the concrete problems of southern farming could claim, with some justice, to propose a solution to the great problem of republican mortality. Taylor's well-run, self-regenerating farm is a metaphor for the well-run commonwealth; further, it is in a completely practical way the foundation for that commonwealth, and its proprietor, the title character of Taylor's book, is the citizen on whom the fortunes of the republic depend.

And so the message of *Arator* is in the end hopeful; Taylor brings up the South's many troubles so he can solve them. The book provides us with two images to contemplate: we see the southern farm as it is, all but ruined by bad farming practices and social institutions; and then we see it as it might be, orderly and prosperous, renewal following on the heels of decay. And most important, we see in considerable detail just how the former image may be transformed into the latter. For Taylor the great joy of farming was that of translating ideals into realities in "a constant rotation of hope and fruition" (313). In *Arator* he displays a reasonable confidence that hope may lead to fruition, that the flawed South of his own day might be "fitted" to the ideal of the South as virtuous pastoral realm. Thus his long list of southern failings—rather like a Puritan jeremiad, though he might not have liked the comparison—implies hope, even promise. The indictment of failure implies the possibility of success, as a photographic negative implies the positive image. We are left with the feeling that the South may yet fulfill its role as the landscape of republican redemption, an image of hope to remind America of its own best aspirations.

At the very end of his life, Taylor again left Hazelwood and returned to the distasteful world of politics, consenting one last time to finish another man's term in the Senate. It was 1822; the nation had just been shocked, during the struggle over the Missouri Compromise, into a sudden awareness of sectional tensions which threatened as nothing had before to pull the republic apart. In his recent book *Construction Construed* (1820), Taylor had written in dismay about this new and dangerous sectionalism, so different, he believed, from his own regional patriotism. When he had spoken, in *Arator* and elsewhere, of the South, he meant the Old South—the tobacco-growing states of Maryland, Virginia, and the Carolinas. He could feel no identification with Missouri, or with the new cotton states of Alabama and Mississippi, already filling up with planters and their slaves, or with the great prize of Texas, on which some southerners had already cast their eyes. Now he was invited to consider these places as somehow contiguous with his own Virginia, and his localist sensibilities rebelled. This "South" was an abstraction, he thought, an artificial union bound together by no "natural interests" but only by the curse of slavery.

Characteristically, Taylor blamed financial speculators, the "paper aristocracy," for stirring up the slavery issue and thus creating this fictional "South," as well as the fictional "North"—farmers of the Old Northwest joined with the merchants of New England—which opposed it. He believed that slavery was a mere pretext for the Missouri dispute; all enlightened people still agreed that slavery was an evil that must be got rid of with all prudent haste, and everyone but a few fanatics could see that this was already being done. The real object of these speculators was to transform a peacefully diverse America, consisting of many regions with many interests, into a battleground dominated by two gigantic antagonists, for convenience labeled "North" and "South." Each of these antagonists would contend in Congress for the power to rule the other; in the end the North would win, and the federal government would proceed unobstructed to enrich Yankee speculators at the expense of southern and western farmers.

In the face of what he conceived as an enormous conspiracy, and what was in any case a firestorm of partisan fury, Taylor in *Construction Construed* calmly offered the old truths of limited government and strict construction. Given the passions the issue ignited, there is something almost awesome about his faith in these old ideas, about the quiet certitude with which he explains, point by point and distinction by distinction, the illegality of the Missouri Compromise. Congress has no power to create a state, he says, but can only admit one, as it already exists, to the Union. The state of Missouri was created by its citizens, whose prerogative it was to write their own state laws; Congress had no more to say about the status of slavery in Missouri than about the same question in Virginia or Massachusetts—nothing at all. Or to reverse the matter, a Congress that could dictate the internal policies of a new state could do the same to the old ones. For Taylor the Missouri Compromise was above all an assault on the autonomy of the states, and it threatened to upset the happily balkanized order which alone permitted the coexistence in America of so many diverse people under a single flag.

Taylor's analysis of the Missouri issue was in certain respects persuasive: no less an authority than Thomas Jefferson declared that a copy of *Construction Construed* should be forced upon every man in Congress.[23] Indeed, it was in certain respects prophetic, for he warned that the sectional contest set in motion by this crisis might end in civil war. But in other respects he badly misjudged the situation. The vast new South which he contemplated in 1820 may have been an artificial creation, but no Yankee speculators were needed to create it. His own fellow southerners—devoted to a pair of institutions Taylor hated, slavery and western expansion—had done it themselves. It would be only ten more years before John Calhoun, in many ways an heir of the southern republican tradition, would identify slavery as "a good—a positive good" and only a few more before southern expansionists began dreaming of a vast empire for slavery.[24] The political world they made—they and their ideological opponents in the North, men like

23. Risjord, *Old Republicans*, 225.

24. John C. Calhoun, "Speech on the Reception of the Abolition Petitions," in *Union and Liberty: The Political Philosophy of John Calhoun*, ed. Ross M. Lence (Indianapolis, 1992), 474. On Calhoun's connection to southern republicanism, see Lacy Ford, "Republican Ideology in a Slave Society: The Political Economy of John C. Calhoun," *Journal of Southern History*, LIV (1988), 405–24.

Garrison and Charles Sumner and Wendell Phillips—was one which Taylor, for all his prescience, could not imagine.

It is scarcely surprising that when, on December 20, 1822, Taylor presented his credentials in the U.S. Senate, assuming political office for the last time, he seemed a noticeably archaic figure. "His whole character was announced in his looks and deportment," remembered Thomas Hart Benton, "and in his uniform (senatorial) dress—the coat, waistcoat, and pantaloons of the same 'London Brown,' and in the cut of a former fashion—beaver hat with ample brim—fine white linens—and a gold-headed cane, carried not for show, but for use and support when walking and bending under the heaviness of the years."[25] He served faithfully until his death two years later, fighting tariffs and loose construction, representing what he considered the interests of Virginia and the South—and in a certain sense, perhaps, representing as well the last generation of Americans for whom the pastoral republican dream of the founding remained a simple and attainable reality.

25. Benton, *Thirty Years' View*, 45.

2

JOHN RANDOLPH AND THE
POLITICS OF DISAPPOINTMENT

John Taylor's usual absence from daily political life was, of course, a considerable loss to the Old Republicans of the South, for he was their leading political theorist. But in fiery, flamboyant John Randolph of Roanoke, Taylor had a political heir and ideological soulmate whose zest for political combat was as strong as his own distaste for it. Like Taylor, Randolph had begun his public career as an ardent Jeffersonian, a hater of John Adams, an advocate of the Doctrines of '98, and a sworn enemy of centralized government. Like Taylor, he eventually broke with Jefferson in the name of pure republican principles and thus chose a life of exile from political power and success, a life spent mainly in warning a heedless America of its descent into corruption. They ought to have made a formidable pair: the calm, disinterested philosopher and the passionate advocate. But Taylor, though he remained a warm friend to Randolph, eventually came to distrust him as a political ally. "Poor Randolph is lost," he wrote to Wilson Cary Nicholas in 1807, "[he is] so blinded by something, supposed to be passion or prejudice, as to have led him into censures of Mr. Jefferson's conduct, in some cases where it is universally approved, and in others upon contradictory grounds, in the opinion of those I have conversed with."[1]

Randolph's volatile personality, his inability to modulate his responses, and his insistence on an ideological purity that struck even Taylor as extreme, made for a fatal disjunction between their two brands of republicanism. It was a disjunction not at the level of doctrine, for they disagreed on few issues of principle, but rather at that

1. Quoted in Risjord, *Old Republicans*, 82.

of strategy—in the broadest sense of the term—of rhetoric. Taylor's suspicions were in order, for Randolph—though he tried perhaps more faithfully than anyone to adhere to the Old Republican vision—none-theless ended by embodying something quite different and in some respects antithetical. As Taylor suspected, Randolph's transformation of the southern republican tradition was largely a matter of style.

Like Taylor, Randolph was the product of an aristocratic Virginia family: political power and responsibility came to him as a birthright. Born at Cawsons, near the mouth of the Appomattox, in 1773, he was a child of the American Revolution, which he came to regard as the high point of his country's moral and political life. Like Taylor, Ran-dolph was exposed early on, both by reading and by contact with the Virginia gentry, to the thought of the Country party; he too absorbed their agrarian economics, their politics of decline and regeneration, their distrust of governmental power, and their personal ethic of virtue and independence. He was educated for the law but soon entered poli-tics, scoring his greatest early triumph in 1799, when, defending the Virginia Resolution in a debate at Charlotte Court House, Virginia, he challenged (and by some accounts defeated) no less an adversary than Patrick Henry. He was elected to Congress a year later, at the age of twenty-six, and quickly made a reputation as a brilliant advocate of Republican positions, becoming within two years his party's leader in Congress.

Randolph was thus a figure of considerable promise, a rare ornament for the Jeffersonian party, as he began his political career. And through-out Jefferson's first term, he made a brilliant and effective congressional leader for his party, displaying considerable tact, judgment, and prac-tical political sense in building support for Republican efforts. But dur-ing the president's second term, Randolph, like the other eventual Tertium Quids, began to doubt Jefferson's dedication to pure republi-canism. After the crisis year of 1805—the year of the Yazoo case and the West Florida bargain—he broke with Jefferson and began a career of violent political opposition to anyone whose republicanism did not measure up to the grand precedent of 1776. Eventually that came to mean virtually everyone in American politics; small wonder Randolph liked to apply to himself a passage from Genesis: "And he will be a wild man; his hand will be against every man, and every man's hand against him."

John Taylor had, of course, chosen a similar political isolation; but Taylor, disgusted with political life, retired to Caroline County, became a respected leader of his community, and above all, as we have seen, undertook what struck him as significant reforming efforts on the depleted soil of Hazelwood. Randolph, fatefully, lacked Taylor's effortless identification with the land and its people. He never found in country life the refuge Taylor discovered there, and he had no taste for the sort of microcosmic reforms in which Taylor found his hope. To be sure, Randolph was nominally a farmer all his life, and for the most part a successful one. He defended agrarian life throughout his public career, and even in private he sometimes tried hard to present himself as a Cincinnatus, most comfortable behind his plow and only reluctantly called away to the emergencies of state. Here, for instance, is Randolph in a letter to Joseph Nicholson, written shortly after his climactic break with Jefferson in 1805: "Thus you see, while you turbulent folks on the east of Chesapeake are wrangling about Snyder & McKean, we old Virginians are keeping it up, *more majorum.* De gustibus non est disputandum, says the proverb; nevertheless, I cannot envy the taste of him who finds more amusement in the dull scurrility of a newspaper than in 'Netherby's Calendar,' and prefers an election ground to a racefield." [2]

But in fact, as most of his letters make plain, Randolph was usually bored by country life and disdainful of country people; he defended the agrarian life eloquently, but he never much wanted to live it. He considered life on his plantation an exile, which he tried unsuccessfully to leaven by making contact with his neighbors: "I have tried to strike root into some of the people around me—one family, in particular; but found the soil too stony for me to penetrate, and, after some abortive attempts, I gave it up—nor shall I ever renew the attempt, unless some change in the inhabitants should take place." The letters are full of acid criticisms of his neighbors' speech, which he considered corrupt, and their manners, which he thought vulgar. Like Taylor, Randolph

2. Quoted in Henry Adams, *John Randolph* (Boston, 1898), 156–57.

was a practitioner of "pastoral politics"; and there is, as Frank Kermode says, an innate irony in the idea of the pastoral: though celebrating life close to nature, it and its author are invariably cultivated products of the city.[3] If Taylor felt any alienation from the simple country life he celebrated, he mitigated it by fully immersing himself in that life, becoming not merely a farmer but perhaps the best farmer in Virginia. But Randolph could never do that, and he felt no real identification with the country people around him. He solved the difficulty of being a pastoral politician largely alienated from pastoral life by identifying himself with an agrarian golden age of the past. Randolph believed that virtuous farmers had once created a nearly ideal republic in America, but for reasons temperamental and ideological, he always felt that this golden age was past and that the present was much diminished. By the time of Jefferson's betrayal of republicanism and the country's benign acceptance of the treason, he was beginning to settle into a habit of pessimism about the American people and their institutions.

This attitude was fateful for a republican of Randolph's sort. For, like Taylor, he believed that a good country could arise only from a virtuous people; even the most ingeniously designed form of government, devised by the shrewdest philosopher, could not make up for the corruption of the citizens. "Republicanism," he wrote in 1801, "depends not on a few orators, statesmen and philosophers, but on the diffusion of general information throughout the whole mass of society."[4] But unlike Taylor, Randolph saw comparatively little hope of reforming the people; also unlike Taylor, he was never seriously tempted to remain on his acres and among those people and thus avoid the crass world of national politics. Corrupt though it was—and no one ever complained more bitterly of its corruption—politics was the arena of ideological conflict, which was Randolph's true home. With the people corrupted, such hope as there was rested with a handful of

3. John Randolph to Dr. Theodore Dudley, December 30, 1821, in *John Randolph of Roanoke: A Study in American Politics*, 3rd ed., ed. Russell Kirk (Indianapolis, 1978), 280; Frank Kermode, Introduction to *English Pastoral Poetry: From the Beginnings to Marvell* (New York, 1972), 14.

4. Quoted in Roger H. Brown, *The Republic in Peril: 1812* (New York, 1971), 148.

men like himself, "orators, statesmen and philosophers," who would do their best to preserve the idea of republicanism—fighting, as T. S. Eliot said, not in the hope of victory but to keep something alive.

As a consequence, Randolph's response to his voluntary exile from the Jeffersonian mainstream was quite different from Taylor's. Lacking his friend's avenue of retreat, he made his stand in Congress and for thirty years waged what amounted to guerrilla warfare against those who would adulterate the republican teachings of his youth. Occasionally he won: he almost single-handedly defeated both the Yazoo compromise and the West Florida scheme. Much more often he stood alone and was, as he sometimes put it, "beaten down horse, foot and dragoons." Eventually he came to expect defeat; eventually, in fact, he came to relish it, seeming to take more pleasure in his lost cause than most of his opponents ever got from winning. But in time the living presence of defeat in Randolph's thought and rhetoric seemed to work a transformation there: the traditional agrarian conservatism he had inherited from his Virginia ancestors became, in his hands, something self-conscious, less a political position than a poetic posture, less a living, prescriptive doctrine than an abstract and personal vision of virtue.

To illustrate this transformation, we might consider a political crisis about which Randolph was particularly passionate and in which he was defeated particularly thoroughly, with fateful consequences for himself and for the nation. This was the coming of the War of 1812, occasioned by repeated British attacks on American shipping. The prospect of war was welcome to many Republicans, particularly to young, expansionist westerners like the Tennessean Felix Grundy, who thought they saw an opportunity for America to seize additional territory. Randolph opposed it, as did other Quids, because he perceived in the aggressive, expansionist attitudes of the war hawks a threat to the small, stable agrarian republic he cherished. And so when he rose in Congress on December 10, 1811, to speak against war—doing so, he said, in spite of "wasted strength and spirits"—he was engaged not only in the immediate task of warning the country away from an unwise policy but in the larger one of reminding it of its proper republican principles, the foundation of its liberty and virtue.[5] A great deal was at stake, and Randolph rose to the occasion, giving what is usually accounted one of his best speeches and what became one of his best-known, something of a model, in antebellum America, of oratorical brilliance.[6] As such, the speech affords a particularly good view of Randolph's characteristic thought and rhetoric and of their relation to the southern republican tradition whose heir he was.

Like most of Randolph's speeches, this one appears utterly chaotic in form; it reads as if he made it up as he went along, which was indeed his usual practice. But in fact the speech presents a reasonably clear argument and does so by an effective method: it circles repeatedly around a single dichotomy, showing it from all angles until its full implication is revealed. "It is a question," Randolph begins, "of *peace* or *war*" (356). But peace and war are not merely the policy alternatives of the moment; as he goes on to demonstrate, they are the expressions of two large and divergent visions of the identity and meaning of America. Like Taylor, Randolph saw this issue—and most others—as a contest between a republican, pastoral vision of America and a tyrannical and commercial one. And, like Taylor, he tended to identify the former vision with the South, the latter with the North—but in 1811, on the issue of war with Britain, it took a considerable rhetorical ingenuity and a certain amount of slick reasoning to maintain the identification. In Randolph's speech, that is, one begins to note a certain slippage between the South as an ideal—the embodiment of the pastoral republican dream—and the South as an actual place.

Randolph begins by setting up the issue in conventional Old Republican terms, pointing out that war would benefit the minority engaged in commerce at the expense of the agrarian majority. "Who will profit by it?" he asks. "Speculators—a few lucky merchants who draw prizes in the lottery—commissaries and contractors. Who must suffer by it? The people. It is their blood, their taxes, that must flow to support

---

5. John Randolph, "Speech Against War with England, December 10, 1811," in Kirk, *John Randolph,* 356. Hereafter cited in the text by page number.

6. Hugh A. Garland, *The Life of John Randolph of Roanoke* (2 vols.; New York, 1850), I, 288.

it" (366). War favored commerce, which for Randolph meant corruption; peace favored "the people," which was to say farmers and planters; it meant preserving an older, pastoral vision of America.

Furthermore, war would require both a standing army and an increased public debt, measures that meant—as the English Country thinkers had taught—the aggrandizement of the central government at the expense of the people's liberty. And it was "a war, not of defence, but of conquest, of aggrandizement, of ambition; a war foreign to the interests of this country, to the interests of humanity itself" (357). It implied an appetite for empire, which would mean the destruction of the republic Randolph cherished—the limited alliance of sovereign states—and the creation of a vast domain, peopled by diverse folk united by no common interests or habits, which could be governed only by the imperial power of Washington. The choice between peace and war, then, was the choice between America as republic and America as empire: in effect, between liberty and slavery. This idea too, of course, was a commonplace among the Tertium Quids.

The conventional next step of the argument was to make the usual identification of republicanism, meaning here the cause of peace, with the South, the most reliably republican section of the country. The trouble was that most of the South passionately favored war with Britain in 1811; it was New England that tended to oppose it. Apparently undaunted by this difficulty, Randolph concedes in passing that most of his southern colleagues, deluded fellows, seem to favor war; then he goes on to explain—with what must be accounted a remarkable inventiveness—that southerners *ought*, if they know their real interests, to agree with him. He spends a bit of time, naturally, reminding the region of its republican heritage; but then to clinch the argument he brings up that most unrepublican of southern institutions, chattel slavery. If war is declared, he says, and if (as expected) the British then invade America, the South will face the prospect of slave insurrections stirred up by the enemy. Why should southerners fear slave revolts now, when there had been none throughout the revolutionary war? Because, Randolph claims, the slaves of the South have lately encountered, and have taken to heart, modern doctrines of liberty and equality. The advocates of these "imprescriptible rights" had taught the slaves "that they were the equals of their masters; in other words, advising them to cut their throats" (372).

It was an odd argument, coming from a southerner who had always identified himself as an "*ami des noirs*" and spent most of his life denouncing the peculiar institution; and it was a farfetched argument as well, since it seems unlikely that very many southern slaves were familiar with the teachings of Jean Jacques Rousseau. Why did Randolph make it? Partly because he was genuinely alarmed by the still recent events of Santo Domingo, where the ideology of republican France really had sparked a bloody race war. But partly, it would appear, because he thought it would work. He was a skillful advocate who knew how to appeal to an audience, and he sensed that nothing would get the attention of southern republicans like a reference to slavery. Randolph said, no doubt sincerely, that he took up the subject "with reluctance" and would touch upon it as tenderly as possible (371). And he changed the subject as quickly as he could, from the issue of slave revolts to the broader one of revolution in general; soon he was launched into a denunciation of Napoleon and a defense of England. The argument was much more an echo of Edmund Burke—an old hero to Randolph and other Quids—than it was a forecast of the proslavery fire-eaters of a later day. But still the case is remarkable. Taylor and other southern republicans had occasionally defended slavery against what they considered irresponsible attacks on it, but they always spoke of the institution as a threat to republican order, not an ally. Randolph thought of it the same way, but in this impassioned speech, for a brief moment at least, he was led by rhetorical necessity to yoke the cause of republicanism to the defense of slavery.

This one oddity aside, Randolph's speech was conventional Tertium Quid fare, a defense of a traditional, agrarian society against the threat of radical change. But isolating the content of this speech is not the same as understanding its full significance. That is no doubt true of any forensic performance, but it seems particularly true of Randolph's, for few public figures in American history have displayed such distinctive rhetorical mannerisms, which carried a meaning of their own. In this particular speech, I shall argue, style and content were virtually at war with each other.

What can we say of Randolph's rhetoric? A few quotations may suffice to suggest his characteristic style, in this speech and in general. Here he is, for example, on that "wild project of mad ambition" (358), American expansionism: "I can almost fancy that I see the Capitol in motion towards the falls of Ohio—after a sojourn taking its flight to the Mississippi, and finally alighting on Darien; which, when [the expansionists'] dreams are realized, will be a most eligible seat of Government for the new Republic (or Empire) of the two Americas!" (365). Here, on his opponents' confident plan of waging war against Britain by invading a supposedly hospitable Canada: "But it seems this is to be a holiday campaign—there is to be no expense of blood, or treasure, on our part—Canada is to conquer herself—she is to be subdued by the principles of fraternity. The people of that country are first to be seduced from their allegiance, and converted into traitors, as preparatory to making them good citizens" (365). And on the prospects of such a campaign: "Go! March to Canada! Leave the broad bosom of the Chesapeake and her hundred tributary rivers—the whole line of seacoast from Machias to St. Mary's unprotected! You have taken Quebec—have you conquered England? Will you seek for the deep foundations of her power in the frozen deserts of Labrador?" (368). And on America's perverse antipathy to Britain: "Strange! that we should have no objection to any people or Government, civilized or savage, in the whole world. The great Autocrat of all the Russias receives the homage of our high consideration. The Bey of Algiers and his Divan of Pirates are very civil, good sort of people, with whom we find no difficulty in maintaining the relations of peace and amity—'Turks, Jews and Infidels'; Mellimelli; or the Little Turtle; Barbarians and savages of every clime and colour are welcome to our arms. . . . Name, however, but England, and all our antipathies are up in arms against her" (374). The advocates of war are in the grip of a "mania" (358)—the right treatment for them, he asserted on another occasion, was "a straight-waistcoat, a dark room, water, gruel, and depletion."[7] They claim to be Republicans, but in truth these *de facto* allies of Napoleon "give no other proof of their progress in Republicanism,

7. Quoted in Adams, *John Randolph*, 173.

except a blind devotion to the most ruthless military despotism that the world ever saw" (375). Randolph's rhetoric, here and in general, is grandiloquent, exclamatory, by turns hyperbolic, sarcastic, and openly abusive of all who disagree, which in this case meant virtually everyone listening to his speech. It is a rhetoric calculated to win attention, no doubt, but almost to repel sympathy or agreement. In fact, Randolph's rhetorical excesses, coupled with his apparently rambling, disconnected logic, might have led (and often did lead) his auditors to suppose that he was a bit out of his head. And Randolph himself, perversely, appears to encourage this suspicion: he complains throughout this speech of his mental and physical exhaustion and concludes by regretting that "my bodily indisposition has obliged me to talk perhaps somewhat too wildly; yet I trust that some method will be found in my madness" (379).

Suppose we take him at his word for a moment. If there was a method in Randolph's madness, what might it have been—what purpose was served by his extravagant style? "To the hard-of-hearing you shout," said Flannery O'Connor once, explaining why she found the sensational and grotesque useful in communicating her religious vision to modern readers. Certainly the impression one gets, reading Randolph's speeches, is of a man shouting—shouting, most often, at Republicans who had forgotten their political tradition. The controlling rhetorical strategy of this speech is repeatedly to raise the question, "Who is a genuine republican?" The question, of course, referred to much more than party membership: it meant, "Who upholds republican values?"—or, more broadly, "Who has preserved political virtue?"

Who were the true republicans? Not, Randolph makes clear, most of those who claimed the name. Not westerners like Grundy, who supported war out of greed for empire. Not northerners, who coveted the economic profits war would bring. Not even southerners, though the South, Randolph liked to believe, virtually embodied republicanism: most southern congressmen, favoring war as strongly as their northern and western counterparts, likewise failed the test.

Where was genuine republicanism to be found? Primarily in the past: Randolph refers repeatedly in this speech to the superior republican virtue of an earlier America, one that had repeatedly eschewed war despite much greater provocations than those of the present crisis. And despite evidence to the contrary, it *was* to be found in the South—not the South that had sent a large delegation of war hawks to Congress, but another, more virtuous South, one somehow almost unrepresented in Washington, its preferences made articulate only by John Randolph. "Virginia planters will not be taxed to support such a war," he insists (378), stubbornly ignoring the manifest war fever of his own Virginia constituents, who would shortly punish his pacific efforts by voting him out of office. Randolph's peace-loving Virginia planter, locus of pure republican sentiments, is more an imaginary ideal than an actual citizen.

By 1811, Randolph was able to find republican virtue mainly in his own memory and imagination—faculties which, in his profoundly nostalgic mind, were nearly indistinguishable. The exception to his general condemnation of his times, the one living Virginian who fully embodied the virtues of the idealized past, the idealized South, was of course himself; needless to say, true republicanism was to be found in John Randolph. Throughout the speech he scathingly compares the counterfeit republicanism of his enemies to his own *bona fides*. To the question, "Who is a republican?" his final answer is essentially "I am, and practically no one else."

Unlike some of Randolph's later speeches, this one is not primarily a meditation on his own existence, on the meaning of being John Randolph. But there is implicit in it, nonetheless, a rather melancholy self-portrait: he is isolated and alone, the last living repository of republican virtue, inevitably alienated from the corrupt political world around him. It is not surprising that he felt that way, for by now virtually no one in Congress shared his aversion to war with Britain. Even his fellow southerners could now be appealed to only in the name of slavery, not that of republicanism. "I listen to the wisest of them," Randolph said of his colleagues, "& to me their talk is as the talk of children. I do not pretend to argue with them, for I speak a language which they cannot understand."[8] Thus, presumably, the need to shout: with argument precluded, how else could he make his presence felt?

8. Quoted in Brown, *Republic in Peril*, 154.

How else could one so far from the mainstream be heard? Thus too, it would seem, the odd admission of madness. Randolph made that admission fairly often, and sometimes it was literally true, but frequently, as Robert Dawidoff has shown, it was a deliberate pose, meant to add rhetorical emphasis to his ongoing critique of modern America. Here as elsewhere, the pose stresses Randolph's isolation and alienation, which, given the corrupt political circumstances in which he lived, he considered the stigmata of his anachronistic virtue. "I have lost my grasp upon the world," he wrote in 1825. "If it be not mad, then I am."[9]

All of this suggests that Randolph, in this speech and elsewhere, was involved in an uncomfortable paradox. He spoke for republican orthodoxy, for a vision of an old-fashioned, peaceful, integrated society, just as John Taylor had. But he spoke for this vision in a language which, by its clear implication, tended to undermine it. He spoke for traditional Whig virtue in the idiom of modern romanticism: his stance as the lone rebel, half-mad and defying the world, recalls one of Randolph's favorite writers, Lord Byron. He urged the virtues of community with a rhetoric of profound alienation—defending, to an indifferent world, a lost republican community of which he was the last living member. He undertook to defend a social order that claimed to be the antithesis of abstraction, and he did so by making an abstraction of it—not the South as it actually was, marred by expansionism, war fever, and greed, but the South as it ought to be, the *idea* of the South. Doctrine and rhetoric pull stubbornly against each other in Randolph's speech, in a tension that was, perhaps, one source of his famously spellbinding oratorical power.

One doubts that the implicit apostasy of Randolph's language was deliberate. But he was confronted with a formidable rhetorical problem. He was the heir of an emphatically empirical, nonabstract body of political doctrine, which existed, or claimed to exist, not in the minds of philosophers but in the lived experience of virtuous citizens.

9. See Robert Dawidoff, *The Education of John Randolph* (New York, 1979); Randolph to Dr. John Brockenbrough, July 8, 1825, in *The Collected Letters of John Randolph of Roanoke to Dr. John Brockenbrough, 1812–1833,* ed. Kenneth Shorey (New Brunswick, 1988), 57.

Those citizens and their institutions were—as in *Arator*—the objective correlatives of the doctrine, the images that constituted its only legitimate expression. But Randolph had been tending for years toward the belief, which the nation's eagerness for war only confirmed, that these virtuous citizens were scarcely to be found anymore, that their institutions were dying. How was he to frame his vision when there was nothing to sustain it, when it had become a pure idea with no empirical reality to base itself on? The rhetoric of his antiwar speech may be taken, I think, as a provisional answer to the question: the solution, if there was one, lay in Randolph's own mind and rhetoric, in his capacity to *imagine* the political symbols that were no longer available in reality.

Randolph elaborated upon this provisional solution, ingeniously but at considerable cost, during what might be called the second half of his public career. The first half came to an end not long after his speech of December 10, when because of his opposition to a popular war he lost his seat in Congress and returned in painful exile to his Roanoke plantation. This political defeat marked the beginning of a particularly dark period of Randolph's life, a span of barely two years which saw financial trouble for his plantation, the death of one beloved nephew and the mental breakdown of another, and—by some accounts—a bout of insanity for Randolph himself. And his personal tragedy seemed reflected in the condition of the state and nation, a Virginia wracked by economic depression, an America invaded by foreign troops, its Capitol in flames. In 1814 Randolph made a trip to his birthplace at Cawsons, found it ruined, and saw in the wreckage an emblem of the fate of the Virginia and the America of his youth; his several letters about the experience all have the tone of this one to Thomas Forman: "I made a late visit to my birthplace. At the end of a journey through a wilderness, I found desolation & stillness as if of death—the fires of hospitality long since quenched—the hearth cold—& the parish church tumbling to pieces, not more from natural decay than sacrilegious violence. This is a faithful picture of this state from the falls of the great river to the sea-board." Simultaneously his sporadic efforts to discover some lingering virtue among his neighbors, to "strike root" in the people around him, came to an end: "For weeks together I never see a new face," he wrote to Francis Scott Key, "and to tell you the truth, I am so much of Captain Gulliver's way of thinking respecting my fellow Yahoos (a few excepted, whose souls must have transmigrated from the generous Houyhnhnms), that I have as much of their company as is agreeable to me."[10] As might be imagined, Randolph's letters during the war years are full of such despairing observations. Perhaps inevitably, his habitual pessimism about himself and his country deepened during this period.

And if the war began the job of sealing Randolph as a pessimist, the peace completed it. Of course, the country survived the War of 1812, even salvaging a measure of pride thanks to Andrew Jackson's triumph at New Orleans. The Republican party did more than survive, becoming by 1816 not just the dominant but the only national political organization. Randolph himself survived and was soon restored to his seat in Congress. It was for most Americans the Era of Good Feelings, but John Randolph became a more intransigent oppositionist than ever. It was an age of territorial expansion, but Randolph continued to warn against the lure of empire and to state the case for a small republic; he boasted that he had never voted to admit a new state to the Union. It was an age of increasing democracy, with manhood suffrage becoming the rule in most places, but Randolph fought to restrict Virginia's franchise to the property holders who, as his Country principles taught, were the only reliable citizens. It was a time of industrialization and of expanding federal power, the two tendencies coming together in the American System of tariffs, the National Bank, and federally funded internal improvements: but Randolph still preached the gospel of agriculture and states' rights, bitterly opposing the American System and its architect, Henry Clay.

But though he fought these measures, he was forced to concede that it was largely a losing battle. The decline of pastoral republicanism and the corresponding gains of expansionism, industrialism, and federal power signified for Randolph the loss of republican virtue on the part

10. Quoted in Jay B. Hubbell, *The South American Literature* (Durham, 1954), 223; Randolph to Francis S. Key, July 17, 1813, in Garland, *John Randolph*, II, 16.

of the people, North and South. In 1814 he remembered—in a mood of pronounced nostalgia—the republican planters of an older Virginia: "The proprietors were generally well educated—some of them at the best schools of the mother country, the rest at William and Mary, then a seminary of *learning,* under able classical masters. Their habitations and establishments,—for the most part spacious and costly, in some instances displayed taste and elegance. They were the seats of hospitality. The possessors were gentlemen, better bred men were not to be found in the British dominions."[11] But here was the present state of the Virginian as *zoon politikon:* "We hug our lousy cloaks around us, take another chaw of tubbaker, float the room with nastiness, or ruin the grate and fire irons, where they happen not to be rusty, and try conclusions upon constitutional points."[12] He still believed, as he had all along, that the political order of the country depended upon the citizens: "In the virtue, the moderation, the fortitude of the people," he said in 1815, "is (under God) our last resource. . . . None but the people can forge their own chains."[13] But by 1815 Randolph had come to believe less than ever in "the people."

The postwar rage for expansion sparked what was for Virginia and the South the most ominous political crisis of all: the Missouri dispute of 1819, during which the issue of slavery first began to exert its divisive force. Randolph's attitude toward slavery was as ambiguous as everything else about him. It is clear that as a young man, full of the spirit of the French Revolution, he pronounced himself an *ami des noirs* and attacked slavery as a violation of the rights of man. Even in later years, when revolutionary passion had given way to Burkean conservatism, he continued to declaim against the institution: in 1815 he delivered a speech against the domestic slave trade which, as Russell Kirk says, "Garrison would not have hesitated to publish."[14] Randolph, however, was himself a slaveholder. He had inherited a large number of slaves

11. Quoted in Robert Dawidoff, *The Education of John Randolph* (New York, 1979), 207.

12. Randolph to John Brockenbrough, November 15, 1831, in *Collected Letters,* ed. Shorey, 138.

13. Quoted in Dawidoff, *Education,* 220.

14. Kirk, *John Randolph,* 168.

from his father, whose estate was so encumbered by debt that Randolph was never able to free them during his lifetime, though he did so by a provision of his will. And though he attacked the institution in general, Randolph was capable of idealizing his relations with his own slaves, whom he consistently identified as his dearest friends. Eventually—beginning roughly at the time of the Missouri crisis—he came to consider northern hostility toward slavery as much a danger to republican order as was the institution itself. He believed that northern abolitionists were ignorant and fanatical, and he accepted without question the almost universal southern assumption that sudden and general emancipation would probably lead to racial warfare. At times he expressed the hope that slavery, as it became more and more unprofitable, would slowly disappear on its own; at other times he put his faith in the various private efforts to emancipate slaves and settle them outside the South, in the western territories or in Liberia. And at times, during his many periods of inconsolable gloom, he seemed to regard the problem as hopelessly insoluble.

But whatever his private attitude toward the institution, it is clear that Randolph exploited it rhetorically to win support for his political efforts. This was evident as early as his 1811 speech against war, when he identified the South with the cause of peace by numbering the threat of slave revolt among the consequences of war. Later he exploited southerners' tender feelings about the issue by identifying the defense of slavery with his own cherished cause of states' rights—an identification which Henry Adams considered Randolph's chief contribution to American politics. No doubt Randolph was much more worried about federal power than about the emancipation of slaves, which he continued to regard as a desirable outcome. But when acting as a practical politician—an identity that never fully receded—he knew that the way to get the South's attention was to warn of a threat to slavery. What this meant, of course, was that the slave system, not pastoral republicanism, was now the defining feature of southern political culture. For Randolph it was certainly a disfigurement—a "cancer," as he often called it—but politics forced him to recognize its presence. This development must have been a bitter one for a man whose lifelong habit was to identify the South with the purest repub-

licanism. But if so, it was consistent with most of the developments of
the Era of Good Feelings, all of which deepened his already considerable pessimism about the political and moral world in which he moved.

How, in such a debased world, was he to frame his continuing protest
against the tendencies of the age? Robert Dawidoff, in a splendid book
on Randolph, offers the beginning of an answer: "In his last years," he
reports, "Randolph abandoned himself to the character known as 'Randolph of Roanoke,' the eccentric and prophetic figure of the old-
fashioned times which democratic America was fast supplanting."
"Randolph of Roanoke," Dawidoff explains, was in effect an exaggera-
tion, almost a caricature, of the real John Randolph. No one knows,
of course, to what extent this figure was a deliberate creation, but most
students of Randolph's career have suspected that there was considerable self-consciousness in his public image. Hugh Blair Grigsby, writing
of his friend only a few years after his death, praised him as "a consum-
mate actor. In the philosophy of voice and gesture, and in the use of
pause, he was as perfect an adept as ever trod the boards of Covent
Garden or Drury Lane." Thomas Hart Benton judged that Randolph's
"keen, refined, withering sarcasm" was for him "a lawful parliamentary
weapon to effect some desirable purpose"; and Henry Adams agreed
that "his insulting language and manner came from the head and not
the heart; they were a part of his system, a method of controlling his
society as he controlled his negroes." But Dawidoff has gone furthest
in this direction. Noting Randolph's strong taste for imaginative literature—something of an eccentricity among Virginians of his day—
he suggests that "if Randolph read for any profession, it was the profession of the imagination." Though he never wrote anything but letters, Randolph considered himself a man of poetic temperament.
"Shakespeare and Milton," he wrote to his nephew Theodore Dudley,
"and Chaucer and Spenser and Plutarch and *The Arabian Night's En-
tertainments* and *Don Quixote* and *Robinson Crusoe* and 'the tale of Troy
divine' have made up more than half of my worldly enjoyment."[15] His

15. Dawidoff, *Education*, 242, 125; Grigsby quoted in William Cabell Bruce, *John
Randolph of Roanoke, 1773–1833* (2 vols.; New York, 1922), II, 95; Benton, *Thirty*

one great literary creation, Dawidoff concludes, was his own public persona, the eccentric but formidable figure who, year after year, paced the floor of the House of Representatives, brilliantly excoriating the republic for its iniquities.

Who was "Randolph of Roanoke," and what purpose did he serve for his creator? A passage from Benjamin Perley Poore's *Reminiscences of Sixty Years in the National Metropolis* (1886) offers a good portrait of Randolph in this congenial role:

> He used to enter the Senate Chamber wearing a pair of silver spurs, carrying a heavy riding whip, and followed by a favorite hound, which crouched beneath his desk. He wrote, and occasionally spoke, in riding gloves, and it was a favorite gesture to point the long index-finger of his right hand at his opponent as he hurled forth tropes and figures of speech at him. Every fifteen minutes, while he occupied the floor, he would exclaim in a low tone, "Tims, more porter!" and the assistant doorkeeper would hand him a foaming tumbler of potent malt liquor, which he would hurriedly drink, then proceed with his remarks, often thus drinking three or four quarts in one afternoon.[16]

Randolph had for years been a singularly unsuccessful politician, but now—playing Randolph of Roanoke—he began to exult in his failure, a failure that simply proved his stubborn independence and virtue. He identified himself as a Cassandra, a Quixote, as "the warder on the lonely hill"; he boasted that he had stood siege "against the whole power and patronage of the Government" and opined that "to fall in such a cause was no mean glory."[17] Set upon by political enemies in Congress, he defiantly quoted King Lear: "The little dogs and all, Tray, Blanch and Sweetheart, see, they bark at me!"[18] Nearly his first act upon returning to Congress was to publish an open letter to his con-

---

Years' View, 473; Adams, *John Randolph*, 259; letter to Dudley quoted in Dawidoff, *Education*, 120.

16. Benjamin Perley Poore, *Perley's Reminiscences of Sixty Years in the National Metropolis* (2 vols.; Philadelphia, 1886), I, 68–69.

17. Randolph to John Brockenbrough, December 23, 1821, in *Collected Letters*, ed. Shorey, 40; Dawidoff, *Education*, 235.

18. Bruce, *John Randolph*, I, 430.

stituents, notifying them of his indifference to their approval: he would
follow his principles, popular or not.

This loudly asserted independence found expression too in Randolph's increasingly eccentric manner. He had always been unconventional, of course, but now he exaggerated his eccentricity in ways evidently meant to draw attention to it. Sometimes he dressed, as Poore
noted, in hunting clothes and brought his hounds onto the floor of
Congress with him; other times he made a point of wearing what he
called "Revolutionary blue and buff," meant to recall the uniform of
the Continental army. Likewise, it was during these years that Randolph became famous for his scathing epigrams, even getting credit for
the humor of others. "All the bastard wit of the country is fathered
upon me," he eventually complained. Robert Livingston was "a man
of splendid abilities, but utterly corrupt. Like a rotten mackrel by
moonlight, he shines and stinks"; Jefferson was always "St. Thomas of
Cantingbury"; and the alliance of John Quincy Adams and Henry Clay
was "the coalition of Blifil and Black George . . . the combination,
unheard of till then, of the Puritan with the Blackleg." With these
deliberate insults—the last of which provoked a famous duel with
Clay—Randolph was asserting, and thus reminding the country, of the
republican gentleman's independence, his freedom from cant and his
willingness to speak even unpopular truths when necessary. With his
various outlandish costumes he was suggesting the healthy virtue of
the landed republican gentleman, the romantic dash of the southern
cavalier, and the all-but-vanished patriotism of the founding generation. Just as Dawidoff says, Randolph of Roanoke was a shrewdly
constructed "figure of the old-fashioned times." One might even say
that Randolph anticipated the European intellectual tradition of the
"dandy," of the self-consciously alienated figure who, says T. John Jamieson, "found that the best argument (and the most violent protest)
was simply to embody his own ideal."[19] Randolph of Roanoke, clad in
his revolutionary blue and buff, boasting of his independence and re-

19. Quoted in Dawidoff, *Education*, 63; Gerald W. Johnson, *Randolph of Roanoke:
A Political Fantastic* (New York, 1929), 16–17; T. John Jamieson, "Conservatism's
Metaphysical Vision: Barbey d'Aurevilly on Joseph de Maistre," *Modern Age*, XXIX
(1985), 31.

sistance to corruption, was a deliberate embodiment of the principles America was abandoning. He was a walking reproach to the rest of the country, an image of the better world the people had rejected.

We have already noted the difficulties Randolph encountered in trying to articulate his republican vision in an America where he alone seemed to value that vision, indeed even to remember it. Randolph of Roanoke, the logical terminus of his forced retreat into memory and imagination, was a brilliant solution to the problem. By self-consciously embodying his own ideals—republicanism, the past, the South—Randolph took the hard necessity imposed by his situation and made a virtue of it. If, discussing true republicanism, he inevitably found himself discussing John Randolph of Roanoke, then Randolph of Roanoke would become a figure worth discussing, a Cassandra, a Quixote, a Lear, or a Byron. If the only available symbol of political virtue was himself, then a symbol he would become, and a memorable one. Anglo-American republicanism had always depended on the idea of "virtual representation," whereby a good statesman was said genuinely to represent even constituents who had not voted for him so long as he honestly pursued their true interests. Randolph was invoking this idea in extreme form when claiming that he in his lonely opposition represented the real interests of the country. But in his hands this political idea elided into an essentially literary one: representation became metaphor, and the representative became—more or less in Emerson's sense—the representative man, claiming to represent not just interests but ideals. Randolph would no doubt have been uncomfortable in the company of Emerson's American Scholar or Whitman's American poet, and it is hard to imagine what he would have made of Emerson and Whitman themselves. But in a certain sense he was their ancestor, an intellectual who found power in his very alienation from power, who managed by sheer assertion, by dramatically personifying his defeated ideals, to make his presence felt by an age that would have preferred to ignore him.

The created character Randolph of Roanoke, that is, served as the objective correlative of John Randolph's political and moral vision. It served for him the same purpose that the well-managed Virginia farm served for John Taylor, as an emblem of embattled values—republicanism, the pastoral, the South. But between these two controlling images there are enormous differences despite the ideological similarities that underlay them. The meaning of Taylor's metaphor was inextricably bound up in its literal reality. The well-managed farm, preserving itself by the natural cycle of decay and regeneration, was for Taylor something real and three-dimensional; indeed, he lived there. And it was no mere symbol of political, social, and personal regeneration: it was the agent and the *sine qua non* of those developments as well. Taylor knew, by painstaking empirical inquiry, that the Virginia farm could be restored; thus he believed that America's social, political, and personal morality could likewise be reformed. For all Taylor's own temperamental grouchiness and pessimism, his image of the good society cannot help but be an image of hope: in principle, the good society Taylor represents in *Arator* is achievable.

But the meaning of Randolph of Roanoke, Randolph's corresponding metaphor of political and personal virtue, is altogether different. To begin with, much of the point of Randolph of Roanoke is his determined unreality: one of his biographers calls him a "political fantastic," which seems accurate enough. Randolph of Roanoke was as exotic and otherworldly as Taylor's Virginia farm was common. A Virginian might reasonably adopt Taylor's four-shift farming method and thus do his part to reestablish the virtue of his country, but he could hardly be expected to assume the mannerisms of Randolph of Roanoke. The prosperous farm was a possibility, but Randolph of Roanoke was emphatically impossible: he was meant to be. He was the last virtuous man, the emblem of ideals not just endangered but utterly vanquished, beaten down horse, foot, and dragoons. Taylor's thought was a dynamic conservatism, a politics of decay and regeneration; but Randolph's was a reactionary romanticism, a self-consciously hopeless nostalgia for times irretrievably vanished. In Taylor's moral world, as on the good farm that was its central symbol, one might yet achieve an "accommodation between our ideas and operations": republican ideals were still connected, if tenuously, with American practice. For Randolph there yawned an unbridgeable chasm between them, between the image of the good society—contained in the past and in one man's lively memory of it—and the present reality of irreversible decline.

All of this points to a final difference between Taylor's political symbolism and Randolph's. Taylor locates his image of virtue in the practical, contemporary world: it is something embodied by existing (albeit neglected) social institutions, something that has its being in history. But Randolph's emblem of virtue, in its otherworldliness, its calculated impossibility, its general hopelessness, finds its home not in the world, not in history, but in the mind of John Randolph. In Randolph's thought the republican pastoral tradition is no longer a living body of social prescription, inherited wisdom embodied in the daily lives of good citizens. Now it has become an abstract idea, to be looked for not in the practices of a hopelessly corrupt society but only in the mind of an eccentric, alienated intellectual.

This transformation, in the hands of later southern intellectuals, made possible a remarkable level of abstraction in the articulation of southern thought. Randolph, perhaps following Burke, remained a hater of abstractions and would have denied vehemently that he was purveying them; and indeed, compared to such later metaphysicians of southern identity as George Fitzhugh, his was a concrete mind. But Randolph anticipated them in his tendency to make the South as much an idea as an actual place. John Taylor spoke for the South too, at least for the part of it he knew, the tobacco-growing states of the Atlantic seaboard; and he employed the region as a symbol of certain social virtues. But it is hard to read *Arator* and doubt Taylor's essential grounding in the concrete reality of the South as well as its symbolic significance. He was able to hold both the idea and the reality of the South simultaneously in mind and to believe that the two might at some point converge. How little hope Randolph had of that convergence may be seen in his remarkable, apocalyptic 1829 letter to John Brockenbrough: "The country is ruined past redemption: ruined in the spirit and character of the people. The standard of merit and morals has been lowered far below '*Proof*.' There is an abjectness of spirit that appalls and disgusts me. The whole South will precipitate itself upon Louisiana and the adjoining deserts. Hares will hurdle in the Capitol. 'Sauve qui peut' is my maxim. Congress will liberate our slaves in less than twenty years. Adieu." [20] Randolph seems to have despaired of the actual South

20. Randolph to John Brokenbrough, January 12, 1829, in *Collected Letters*, ed. Shorey, 117.

and to have pinned his hopes on the idea—an idea he increasingly identified with himself. His career is as pure an example as we are likely to find of what Lewis Simpson has called the "inwardness of history."[21]

At times, of course, Randolph was forced to confront the distance between the idealized South, represented by himself, and the region where he actually lived—and never more notably than when, in 1821, he came to write his will. "I give to my slaves their freedom," reads its first sentence, "to which my conscience tells me they are justly entitled."[22] The document also provided the freed slaves with considerable property in Ohio, where Randolph expected them to establish themselves as farmers. Like so many of Randolph's actions, this last one was self-consciously public and exemplary: he expressed the wish that his will would point a way for Virginia to purge the cancer of slavery. It was a deeply significant and in many ways a hopeful gesture. To provide freed slaves with landed property was to include them in the pastoral republican vision which Randolph had defended all his life; it was to imagine for them—in the future if not the present—a place in the American garden. But at the same time Randolph's gesture was an acknowledgment that his own region was so marred by racism and slavery that it could provide no permanent home for freed slaves, even freed slaves transformed into republican farmers. The redemption of the pastoral republican ideal would take place, if at all, somewhere outside the South.

It turned out, of course, that the Old Northwest—which would soon hatch the republican but frankly racist Free Soil party—offered little more hope than Randolph's Virginia. He did not live to see the outcome of his gesture, when his former slaves, trying to take possession of their Ohio lands, were met with violence and driven away by white settlers. But it might not have surprised him; very little ever did, and he was long since accustomed to seeing his dream, the pastoral dream of America and the South, frustrated. "Remorse," the story goes, was the word he repeated over and over, on his deathbed in 1833.

21. Lewis P. Simpson, *The Fable of the Southern Writer* (Baton Rouge, 1994), 1–12.
22. Quoted in Garland, *John Randolph*, II, 149.

3

NATHANIEL BEVERLEY TUCKER AND THE HISTORICAL ROMANCE OF THE FUTURE

Given Randolph's carefully cultivated public image of noble failure, it might be accounted the crowning irony of a studiedly ironical life that his last political act was a success. This was his effort, just four years before his death, to resist what he considered destructive changes in the Virginia Constitution. At the 1829 Constitutional Convention Randolph led the triumphant conservatives, as he had once led the Tertium Quids in defeating the Yazoo compromise and the West Florida bargain. The worst constitutional changes were averted, and the speeches Randolph made at the convention, despite his advanced age and desperately bad health, were among the most brilliant of his career. But even here he presented himself in the usual way: he was the last virtuous man, hopelessly trying once more to hold back the encroaching tide of barbarism. And despite this triumph, there is nothing in his subsequent career to indicate that cheerfulness was breaking in. By this time defeat had become so accustomed that, when victory was at hand, Randolph seemed scarcely to recognize it.

And yet victory, of a sort, was finally at hand for Randolph and his colleagues: by the time of his triumph at the Virginia convention, his chronic hopelessness might have seemed a bit out of place, for the South, beginning at about the time of the Missouri crisis, had begun at last to attend the warnings of the Old Republicans. There was nostalgia now for the political ideas that had once resisted John Adams: they might, it was felt, resist the new northern efforts to contain and eventually eradicate slavery. By 1824, says William J. Cooper, "the South overwhelmingly desired a return to the 1790's, ideologically and politically."[1] And so during this period Taylor, Randolph, and the other Old Republicans—having spent their lives as an embattled minority—suddenly found themselves transformed into southern heroes. James M. Garnett described this astonishing development to Randolph in 1819: "*You* were toasted lately by a public meeting in Prince George [County] where there were some men present who, but a few short years before, would probably have seen you *roasted* as soon as drink your health. . . . [John Taylor] too is now eulogised to the skies by many who not long since would have thought it a national blessing for him to be hanged." Even Jefferson, whom Taylor had criticized and Randolph had flayed mercilessly, now mended his fences with these old adversaries: he wrote the Richmond editor Thomas Ritchie in 1820 that "Colonel Taylor and myself have rarely, if ever, differed in any political principle of importance"; and in 1824 he named Randolph and several other Quids as his "companions in sentiments, all good men and true, of primitive principles."[2] The cranks and malcontents who had stayed behind while the Republican party was rolling forward to national power now became prophets, honored at last in their homeland.

Randolph was the particular beneficiary of this abrupt historical revision: having spent his life fashioning himself as a symbol of the southern mind, he lived just long enough to meet a generation of southerners prepared to accept him as such.[3] As early as the Nullification crisis of 1831–1833 John Calhoun, by now the leading spokesman of southern sectionalism, was paying frequent tribute to Randolph as his great political teacher—even though the passionate Virginian and the coldly logical Carolinian were nearly opposite personalities who, when in Congress together, had distrusted each other completely. In 1833, the

1. William J. Cooper, Jr., *Liberty and Slavery: Southern Politics to 1860* (New York, 1983), 154.

2. Risjord, *Old Republicans*, 226.

3. Not that Randolph received the news of his new popularity with any particular enthusiasm. To Brockenbrough on January 19, 1822, he wrote: "Like the long waists of our mothers, I really believe I am growing, if not generally, at least somewhat in fashion. But I hope I am not so old a fool as to presume upon this; for of all fools, an old one is least tolerable" (*Collected Letters*, ed. Shorey, 44).

year of Randolph's death, his nephew Theodore Dudley published, to an enthusiastic southern audience, *Letters of John Randolph to a Young Relative,* a collection of the Chesterfieldian missives he had received throughout his life from his uncle and guardian. Randolph's representative status was sufficiently well established by 1847 that even John Greenleaf Whittier—a Yankee, a Quaker, and an abolitionist, as remote as anyone could have been from southern culture—was able, in "Randolph of Roanoke," to take him as a poetic symbol of the virtues and tragic weaknesses of the slave South. In 1851 the Virginian Hugh Garland published his massive *Life of John Randolph,* which explicitly identified its protagonist as a representative of the southern mind. Most of the southern literary magazines reviewed this book enthusiastically and seized the occasion to repeat its emphasis on Randolph's importance as a representative man. These same journals, throughout the thirty years before secession, published several articles on Randolph: accounts of his struggles in the Virginia convention, personal recollections of his idiosyncrasies, and surveys of his library and reading habits. "It is quite certain," said the *Southern Literary Messenger* in 1858, "that no man was ever more truly Southern in feeling than Mr. Randolph."[4]

Among the southern intellectuals who superintended this revival of Randolph's reputation and of Tertium Quid principles generally, none was more devoted to the man or the cause than a Virginia-born lawyer, college professor, and sometime novelist named Nathaniel Beverley Tucker. He came by his devotion to republican principles naturally enough: he was the son of St. George Tucker, also a lawyer and professor and the author of *A Dissertation on Slavery,* the abolitionist tract I briefly discussed in Chapter 1. The elder Tucker aimed for, and tried to impart to his sons, a vision of republican virtue consisting mainly of stern self-denial and a duty of public service; Beverley spent most of his life trying to live up to that ideal.

His personal devotion to Randolph was perhaps even more natural, for the two were half-brothers—sons of the same mother, Frances Randolph having married St. George Tucker after the death of her first husband. John Randolph was eleven years old when Beverley Tucker

4. "Editor's Table," *Southern Literary Messenger,* XXVI (1858), 396.

was born in 1784. It was just enough of an interval, it seems, to have permitted the eccentric from Roanoke to appear perpetually a hero to his young sibling. When Beverley was fifteen, about to begin his studies at William and Mary, Randolph was defending the Virginia Resolution in debate against Patrick Henry. While the boy sweated over his books and bemoaned the boredom of life in Williamsburg, his half-brother was leading the Jeffersonian faction in Congress, achieving in his mid-twenties a national reputation for brilliance and eloquence. As Tucker began a rather dismal legal career, contending over small claims for smaller fees in the Virginia hamlet of Charlotte Court House, Randolph was dramatically breaking with Jefferson, drawing about himself the mantle of sacred principle, and beginning his career as the defiant Lord Byron of American politics. Even in failure Randolph cut a dashing figure, which Tucker, languishing in a dusty courthouse town, barely able to pay the rent, tried in vain to emulate.

Tucker had good reasons for feeling a failure. Not only did his father and Randolph set formidable precedents, but his brother Henry, just four years older, seemed on his way to living up to them. In the War of 1812, while Beverley drilled with the infantry, never catching a glimpse of the enemy, Henry was winning glory in a cavalry regiment; afterward, while Beverley struggled on in Charlotte Court House, Henry prospered at the bar and served in the state legislature. The younger brother's frustration found its focus, as Tucker's biographer Robert Brugger has pointed out, in his ineptitude as a public speaker: though quick to deride "flippant readiness of speech," he was embarrassed to be a stammerer with no hope of equaling his siblings in oratorical brilliance—the key, in many ways, to success and influence in the Virginia of his day.[5] Like many other young southerners of good birth and education in the first half of the nineteenth century, he felt himself unjustly excluded from the social and political leadership that was, as he had been taught from birth to believe, both his right and his obligation. To achieve influence one must be heard, and it was a "hearing" that Tucker sought throughout his life.

5. Robert J. Brugger, *Beverley Tucker: Heart over Head in the Old South* (Baltimore, 1974), 34.

After struggling for some years in his legal practice, Tucker—now married to the first of his three wives—decided as so many other Virginians were doing to seek a fresh start in the West. His wanderings led him, in 1816, to the Missouri territory, a still unsettled country where an ambitious, well-bred Virginia gentleman could achieve considerable influence. Tucker quickly established himself as a leading lawyer, was soon appointed a territorial judge, and—taking the pen name "Hampden," after the English republican martyr—wrote a series of letters in behalf of states' rights and against the Missouri Compromise. He seemed on his way to achieving in Missouri the prestige and influence that had eluded him in Virginia. Along the way he became involved in the development of Dardenne, a planting community near St. Louis, where he had gathered about him a remarkable group of wealthy and brilliant transplanted southerners; the most notable of them, besides Tucker himself, was William Harper, later chancellor of the University of South Carolina and a prominent defender of slavery. This "slaveholders' Camelot," as Brugger calls it, offered a model of aristocratic life which contrasted strongly with the egalitarian tastes of many other Missourians.[6] In 1820 Tucker made the mistake of publishing in a Virginia paper a "Letter from a Missourian to Virginia," boasting that he and his neighbors at Dardenne had created a true Virginia settlement in the untamed West, a settlement where aristocrats ruled and the common folk gratefully deferred to them. Unfortunately, the letter was reprinted in a St. Louis paper and received hoots and catcalls from the less aristocratic elements of Missouri society. Tucker became the object of considerable democratic resentment, rather as his contemporary James Fenimore Cooper would a few years later in the famous "Fishing Point" episode in New York. Thus did Tucker lose, almost as soon as he had gained it, a good part of his prestige in Missouri.

Tucker had spent sixteen years in the West, buried two wives there, and married a third. Now, under increasing criticism from his neighbors and drawn back east by the death of John Randolph and by the Nullification crisis of 1831–1833, he returned to Virginia and soon as-

6. *Ibid.*, 58.

sumed his father's old professorship at William and Mary. With both Randolph and his father now dead, Tucker felt himself called to take up their labors in behalf of southern republicanism; he began doing so by writing and lecturing on the Nullification issue. Tucker opposed Nullification, finding perverse Calhoun's notion that a state could remain in the Union while defying its laws. Nullification was a halfway measure, he thought: if the Union violated the basic rights of a state, the state ought simply to secede and be done with it. But in these years Tucker believed that President Jackson might remove the need for such a radical remedy by declining to sign the Force Bill then being drawn up in Congress. Traveling to Washington, he actually succeeded in getting an audience with Jackson, engaged the stiff-necked old warrior in arduous debate for several hours, and left believing that he had persuaded him to follow the course of moderation. It was a heady moment for Tucker, though short-lived; this success and the good notices he had won with his essays on Nullification persuaded him that his true calling was that of a political advocate and pamphleteer: "I will never again hold any public employment," he said.[7] Taking up his pen, he began a second career, devoted to persuading his state and nation to return to the republican principles of his ancestors.

Tucker certainly did his best to assume the mantle of these heroes, pouring forth a remarkable torrent of political prose. His first lecture at William and Mary, about the rights of the states in the federal Union, was published as a pamphlet; Tucker sent a copy to Nathaniel Macon of North Carolina, nearly the last survivor of the old Tertium Quid faction, and was gratified to receive the old man's approval. But to modern readers his most interesting works are a pair of novels, both written in a period of a few months in 1836.

Tucker exulted at the speed with which he could churn out fiction; for a time he planned to devote all his energies to fiction writing and eagerly calculated the vast earnings that would come his way once his books began to sell. These expectations were, it turned out, a bit sanguine, and after the two novels of 1836, *George Balcombe* and *The Partisan Leader*, he was to write only one more piece of fiction. But

---

7. Quoted *ibid.*, 90.

these two books were in their way remarkable. *Balcombe*, the story of a young Virginian wandering the Missouri wilderness in search of his lost inheritance, was not without political (and, plainly, autobiographical) significance. But *The Partisan Leader*—a prophetic, futuristic fantasy predicting civil war between North and South—is the book for which Tucker is known today. Written out of loyalty to the pastoral republican creed and a belief that its lessons must be applied to the crisis-ridden politics of the 1830s, *The Partisan Leader* offers one of the best views we have of the pastoral republican mode of thought at a moment of violent transformation in American politics.

In a letter to his brother Henry about the purpose of *The Partisan Leader*, Tucker argued that the old American Union could be preserved only by respect for local diversity and that an effort to make it, as Lincoln would later say, "all one thing or all the other," could succeed only through violence and a radical refounding. In this prediction, we might as well concede, events proved him correct. But in his fantasy of civil war Tucker was also attempting a kind of refounding, not of the whole Union but of the South. No doubt he was attempting, as he told his brother, to bring the wisdom of the Tertium Quids into the present political debates. But he was at the same time calling for the rise of a new, progressive vision of southern identity. Begun, perhaps, as an effort to revive the conservative republicanism of Taylor and Randolph, it quickly became a millennial fantasy, a vision of inevitable progress antithetical to the Tertium Quid notion of southern and American identity.

The novel is set in 1849, some thirteen years in the future. Martin Van Buren (whom Tucker had detested as Andrew Jackson's vice-president and who was about to be elected president when Tucker wrote) is in the novel beginning his fourth term in office. He has continued Jackson's policy of concentrating governmental power in Washington and ultimately in the hands of an imperial presidency and has used this power to raise tariffs, thus enriching America's handful of industrialists at the expense of its great majority of farmers. The southern states, being most abused by this arrangement, have at last seceded from the Union and established a prosperous independent nation—all but Virginia, which has hesitated out of sentimental attachment to the nation it played so large a part in creating. But now a secession movement is beginning in the Old Dominion, which Van Buren seeks to squash by sending his army to occupy the state. Thus begins the struggle that forms the ostensible subject of the novel.

It is within this situation that Tucker constructs his plot, such as it is: outraged by the violation of his state's sovereignty, the novel's hero Douglas Trevor, noble offspring of a distinguished family, raises a band of partisans and sets about liberating Virginia from its oppressors. Along the way he falls in love with and marries his beautiful cousin, befriends a hearty and resourceful backwoods scout, and finds himself at war with his own brother, an officer in Van Buren's army. Such a story might seem to offer at least the prospect of lively action and intrigue, but in fact *The Partisan Leader* offers as little as possible of either—as little as possible, indeed, of most of the conventional elements of the novel. Tucker knows, evidently, that a novel must contain a love story, and so he duly provides one. But whenever a tender moment between Douglas and Delia seems in the offing, the author hurries us past it, impatiently remarking that since the reader can doubtless imagine the scene that ensued, he will not trouble to describe it. As he explains one such occasion, "I am but interested that the reader should understand by what process two principal actors in the scenes of which I am about to speak, were diverted from a zealous devotion to the authority of the United States, in which they had been educated, to a devotion yet more enthusiastic in the cause of Virginia." We hardly need his further disclaimer that "I am not writing a love-tale."[8] Likewise, Tucker knows that a novelist is ordinarily expected to describe his characters, but at certain moments this burden seems too much for him, as when he comes to introduce "the Prime Minister," Van Buren's chief henchman: "No person whose name appears in this history better deserves a particular description than he who now entered. Fortunately I am saved the necessity of going into it, by having it in my power to refer the reader to a most graphic delineation of his exact prototype in

8. Nathaniel Beverley Tucker, *The Partisan Leader: A Tale of the Future* (1836; rpr. Chapel Hill, 1971), 201. Hereafter cited in the text by page number.

person, mind, manners, and principles" (147). Tucker then directs us
to Scott's description of Oliver Dain in *Quentin Durward,* providing
everything but page references. When he could see a shortcut around
tiresome novelistic requirements, Tucker seldom hesitated to take it.
In place of such frivolities as plot and character, he offers mainly a
series of political discussions among the principals, in which the rights
of the states, the grievances of the South, and the abuses of the federal
government are enumerated. So preoccupied is the author with such
questions that he neglects to resolve even the meager story he does
offer. Having written his heroes into a serious bind—Douglas and his
wife, Delia, are both Van Buren's prisoners, with escape apparently
unlikely—Tucker simply ends the novel. Though he is careful to assure
us that Virginia does in the end succeed in its revolution, he does not
trouble to tell us how this was managed, let alone how or even whether
Douglas and Delia were rescued from danger and reunited. Even novelistic closure was an aesthetic flourish which Tucker, with more serious
things on his mind, found that he could forgo.

Not surprisingly, given its shortcomings, the novel received relatively little attention when it appeared in 1836; it was overshadowed
by, among other contemporary titles, the author's own *George Balcombe.* Edgar Allan Poe liked *Balcombe* well enough to regard it "upon
the whole, as *the best* American novel."[9] But *The Partisan Leader* fared
less well. Tucker was forced to pay for its publication, and because of
inadequate distribution, few copies were ever sold; the author apparently realized no profit from it. But understandably it enjoyed something of a rebirth twenty-five years later, when Virginia and ten other
southern states, seemingly following Tucker's script, seceded from the
Union and formed an independent nation. New editions of the novel
were published in both North and South in 1861—in the latter case
to raise morale in the Confederacy, in the former, to prove that secession was the result not of southern hotheadedness but of a long-
premeditated conspiracy against the Union. Both northerners and
southerners, that is, took up *The Partisan Leader* because of its apparent

9. Edgar Allan Poe, "George Balcombe," *Southern Literary Messenger,* III
(1837), 58.

prescience. Contemporary scholars, to the (rather small) extent that they have noticed it at all, have done so for the same reason.

But when it was written, *The Partisan Leader* had at least as much to do with the past as with the future. Its form, the futuristic setting notwithstanding, was that of the historical romance, on the model of Scott's *Waverly* novels. Too, it included among its characters at least a few historical figures in disguise, including John Randolph. Like many other works of futurist fiction—*1984* being the most obvious example—*The Partisan Leader* was among other things a covert analysis of recent history: the history of America's decline, as Tucker saw it, from political virtue. And most important, as I argue below, it was an attempt to adapt anideology borrowed from the past—the system of thought I have been calling pastoral republicanism—to the circumstances of the contemporaneous South. Whether the old Country position could be made to fit the circumstances of the South of the 1830s was, as Tucker knew, a matter of some doubt. The seeming contradiction between them is the main problem which *The Partisan Leader* tries to resolve: "Every document bequeathed to us by history," as Kenneth Burke says, "must be treated as *a strategy for encompassing a situation.*"[10] Among the advantages of recovering this novel is that by probing its strategies—and particularly its flaws, the moments when strategy fails—we can get a sense of what became of the mythology of the pastoral republic in the years leading up to the Civil War. Its shortcomings as a work of art are thus for our purposes almost a virtue: because of the author's single-minded attention to his ideological purposes, his willingness to follow his ideas wherever they led, and his inability to conceal ideological contradictions with formal closure or to dissolve them in sophisticated irony, Tucker's "bad" novel affords an extremely revealing look at what happened to the pastoral republican persuasion in the South as the Civil War approached.

But we ought to begin by making plain what Tucker meant to do and just how his heavy-handed novelistic technique was to help him. *The Partisan Leader* relinquishes its deliberate political meanings with-

10. Kenneth Burke, *The Philosophy of Literary Form: Studies of Symbolic Action* (Baton Rouge, 1941), 109.

out much of a fight: taken as a prediction of the future, the novel begins
as a classical republican's nightmare, the bad dream one might have
after a long evening with Algernon Sidney's *Discourses;* and it ends as
a southern separatist's fantasy. The book's ethical contours are as stark
as any in American fiction; by comparison, *Uncle Tom's Cabin* seems
lost in moral ambiguity. But perhaps it will be well to gloss a few key
scenes and characters, to make it clear just how *The Partisan Leader*
communicates its meanings and indeed how densely packed it is with
cultural information.

The novel is built on a framework of two major plots: a public
action, which is essentially the story of the struggle between Virginia
and the North, and a private action, the internal struggles of the Trevor
family. Beginning with the public action, let us consider the first scene
in the novel. The time is "the latter end of the month of October,
1849" (1), the setting, a small settlement in the foothills of the Blue
Ridge Mountains, where an unidentified horseman appears to survey
the countryside. He beholds a small settlement of farms, "so near to
each other as to allow but a small patch of arable land to each" (1).
Save for a smithy and a small gristmill, there is no sign of manufactures;
indeed, the array of rude log dwellings "betokened an abundance of
timber, and a dearth of everything else" (2). Each cabin has its adjacent
vegetable garden and a small field planted in corn or oats, now awaiting
harvest. "But though the valley thus bore the marks of a crowded
population," Tucker concludes, "a deep stillness pervaded it. The
visible signs of life were few" (3).

Abruptly the rider finds himself surrounded by half a dozen armed
men, "all chiefly clad in half-dressed buckskin" (3). They have apparently been harvesting corn in a nearby field; seeing the approach of a
stranger, they have seized their rifles and come running. "We want a
word with you, stranger, before you go any farther," says one of them
in a "low, quiet tone" (4). An interview ensues between the woodsmen
and the rider, "a handsome youth, about twenty years of age," dressed
in clothing "plain and cheap, but not unfashionable." "His whole air,"
Tucker informs us, "would have passed him for a gentleman, in any
dress and any company, where the constituents of that character are
rightly understood" (5). The woodsmen, it transpires, are members of

Douglas Trevor's partisan band; they wish to know whether the stranger is friend or foe. He converses with them easily, permitting his manner and manly bearing to persuade his questioners, as it soon does, that he is a loyal Virginian and a gentleman. In due course the partisans learn that he is Arthur Trevor, younger brother of their commander, come to help lead them against the enemies of Virginia.

This scene comes directly out of the pastoral republican imagination and is, despite its simplicity, heavily loaded with cultural information. Perhaps the first important fact is simply that, like most others involving the novel's heroic Virginians, it occurs outdoors, as most of those involving Van Buren and his lackeys take place in plush rooms: thus does Tucker insinuate the fundamental distinction between court and country. Too, the scene is that of a community of independent small farmers, in manifest decline. The farmhouses may once have been merely simple and frugal; now they bespeak poverty and deprivation. The autumnal setting suggests imminent decay, though also, of course, the chance of ultimate renewal: in politics as in agriculture, John Taylor had said, renewal must follow on the heels of decay. And the scene at first seems deserted, a detail that would have been lost on no reader familiar with Goldsmith's influential pastoral lament, *The Deserted Village*, or indeed on anyone acquainted with the social pessimism inherent in the pastoral and republican visions. The scene capsulizes, that is, that myth of a lost Eden which helped unite pastoral and republican modes of thought.

The brief exchange between Arthur and the partisans is similarly full of social import. Behind the image of sturdy yeomen taking up arms in defense of their country stands a powerful tradition: Jackson's Tennessee riflemen at New Orleans, the Carolina frontiersmen who won the revolutionary Battle of King's Mountain, Washington's Virginia rangers in the Seven Years' War—and, further in the background, the English republican preference of militia to standing army and ultimately the Roman republican ideal of the *vir bonum*. Later these associations are made clearer when, in the novel's only prolonged battle sequence, we see these partisans fighting from behind rocks and trees and easily defeating the disciplined regulars who have come to suppress them. "The only rule for us is the Indian rule," one of them says (299), instructing us to take these yeomen as the partisans not only of Virginia but almost of nature itself, resisting the corrupt civilization of Van Buren's Washington.

The partisans' recognition of Arthur as a patriot and natural leader is similarly important. Republican thought, because of its deep distrust of power, insisted that ambition was invariably a bad trait in a leader. A desire for power over others would eventually turn a statesman into a tyrant—Tucker's point, after all, about Martin Van Buren. A true leader was someone who did not seek power but had it thrust upon him by the people, against his will if possible. Thus the ritual, observed by political candidates throughout the eighteenth and nineteenth centuries, of insisting that the office in question was a highly unwelcome burden which only their nearly superhuman public-spiritedness could induce them to accept. Nor was the ritual limited to politics; Robert E. Lee, after being offered command of Virginia's armed forces in 1861, began his acceptance by regretting that the legislature had not chosen a worthier man. When Arthur permits the partisans to recognize his merits without prompting, he is demonstrating his freedom from ambition and thus his worthiness to command them.[11]

The characterization of the enemies of these Virginians is equally freighted with moral and political implication. It will be enough to consider briefly Tucker's treatment of Martin Van Buren—a president seldom credited with much in the way of transcendent evil, but here the pure embodiment of tyranny. We invariably see him seated in his "rich and costly" office, dressed in finery, his "egg-bald" head dusted with powder, his dainty hands studded with jewels. From this sanctuary in the White House (now christened "the palace"), he effortlessly administers the corrupt mechanism by which the entire republic has been brought under his personal control. Groveling courtiers come and go, addressing the president as "Excellency" and carrying forth the bribes, threats, and flattering missives by which he guides his apparatus of influence. We learn that he has secured his power by giving office and emolument to corruptible men, by using his standing army and his

11. On this subject, see Kenneth S. Greenberg, *Masters and Statesmen: The Political Culture of American Slavery* (Baltimore, 1985), 1–22.

secret "Court of High Commission" to frighten cowardly ones, and—most diabolical of all—by appealing to the misguided patriotism of the few virtuous folk left, who confuse loyalty to the president with loyalty to the country. The president and his underlings plot openly to subvert the Constitution, intimidate legislators, steal elections, and prosecute innocent men; they frankly refer to the South as "our prey" and discuss how they may more effectively steal its wealth.

The implications of all of this are clear enough. The president is not merely a bad man; he is the embodiment of all the evil which republican thought associated with unchecked power. All the methods of the president—the use of a standing army, of a suborned judiciary, of ingenious constitutional construction, of bribery and the spoils system—had been the stuff of republican paranoia since the seventeenth century. The fear that such methods would be used to enrich "court" at the expense of "country" dates back at least to the eighteenth century and was central to the pattern of thought I have been calling "pastoral republicanism" in the American South.

Thus the public action of the novel. Its significance is reinforced by the private action, concerning the fortunes of the Trevor family. The head of the family, Hugh, is a virtuous old patriot who, though he regrets the pass his country has reached, still remains loyal to the Union and thus to Van Buren. The president has rewarded this loyalty by generously advancing the army career of Hugh's oldest son, Owen, who in turn has become one of Van Buren's most faithful minions. But the second son, Douglas—also an army officer—is of a more independent spirit and, further, has lately come under the influence of his uncle, Hugh's fiery younger brother Bernard. Bernard Trevor is as the world reckons such things rather a failure, with far less of attainment and reputation than his brother; but he has been gifted with a Cassandran prescience that has made him, long before anyone else, an ardent secessionist. Now he has begun educating Douglas in the arcana of this creed.

Van Buren, somehow suspecting that Douglas' loyalty is wavering and improbably anxious to squash this potential enemy, trumps up a charge of treason against the boy and threatens a court-martial. Douglas, it seems, has recently offered to duel another officer (the son of

Van Buren's associate Baker), who in his presence denounced Bernard Trevor and other secessionists. Van Buren knows that the quarrel was not over politics but over young Baker's deliberate insult of Douglas' cousin Delia, daughter of Bernard, who was also present when the remark was made. But he also knows, for he understands the ways of southern gentlemen, that Douglas will be unable to invoke this extenuating circumstance at his court-martial: to do so would require "the public use of a lady's name," an offense scarcely short of murder in the minds of Virginia cavaliers (123). Thus turning the boy's sense of honor against him, Van Buren backs young Trevor into a situation in which he must either resign from the army in disgrace or be convicted: either way, the president thinks, he will be rid of a disloyal subject. Douglas, being himself an honest fellow, is a bit slow in grasping the meaning of all this; but when at last his uncle makes it plain to him, the boy is brought to recognize, in a rapid series of epiphanies, that the president is a scoundrel, that the federal government is corrupt, that membership in the Union will destroy Virginia, and that the state must therefore free itself from tyranny, by force if necessary. Thus begins his career as a partisan.

If the public action of the novel is driven by a contest between power and independence, then this personal plot revolves around a parallel contest between corruption and honor. The significance of this plot depends on our accepting the Trevors, and particularly Douglas, as representatives not only of Virginia ("the destiny of the state depended on him," we hear of the young hero at one point [273]) but indeed of the moral heart of the country: if the Trevors are corrupted or defeated, America's republican spirit will be lost. Accordingly, each family member is a social type, meant to represent one possible response to the rise of tyranny in America. Hugh is a virtuous but somewhat dull-witted republican who allows his reverence for the Union to blind him to its present corruption. Bernard is an equally dedicated republican who, perceiving the danger to liberty more clearly, is able to contemplate radical remedies; he resembles, and was obviously modeled on, Tucker's beloved half-brother John Randolph. Owen Trevor, a beneficiary of the corrupt federal government, has been thoroughly seduced by it and has lost whatever republican and patriotic spirit he may have possessed. Douglas is a young idealist who, after receiving a thorough education in republicanism from his elders, is prepared to restore the lost political virtue of his country. His sense of honor is accordingly his most important characteristic, for what republicanism is to a nation, honor is to an individual: the mark of virtue. That the two went together would have been clear enough to the half-brother of John Randolph, the man who often found that the most expedient way of routing the enemies of republicanism was to duel them. Nor would the point have been lost on any republican reader; all would have agreed that, once the virtue of individual citizens was lost, that of the government would immediately follow.[12]

Thus the importance of Van Buren's rather unlikely means of crushing Douglas. If he can succeed in turning the boy's code of honor against him—if he can make honor a liability in the war against tyranny—Van Buren ensures, if not his own victory, then at least the victory of the corruption he represents. The dramatic question on which this plot turns—whether Douglas will be able to resist Van Buren and keep his honor—represents the larger question posed by the public action of the novel: whether a republic can rescue itself from tyranny.

In 1861 *The Partisan Leader* was taken as a prediction of southern secession. And Tucker himself, in his later years, when he was a passionate secessionist, also came to regard it as such. But this was hindsight; in 1836 his aims were rather more modest. It can be argued, taking the narrowest possible view of Tucker's intentions, that he simply wished to help defeat Martin Van Buren in the election of 1836. The author himself claimed a somewhat broader goal for his work in the letter to his brother which I have already mentioned. "The book was written," he said, "under a belief that the conservation of all that makes the Union valuable, and by the Union itself, depends on the maintenance of the principles of what constituted the old republi-

12. See Bertram Wyatt-Brown, *Southern Honor: Ethics and Behavior in the Old South* (New York, 1982); Dickson D. Bruce, Jr., *Violence and Culture in the Antebellum South* (Austin, 1980); and on the relation between honor and republicanism, Greenberg, *Masters and Statesmen*.

can party of '98, which I would now denominate the States Rights party. . . . In the present state of the periodical press, there is no chance to reach the ear of any mind whose heart and mind are not already with you. I wished a hearing. How was it to be obtained? The idea of the work in question flashed upon me, and in two months it was in the printer's hands." [13] His book, then, was meant to dramatize the need for a recovery of Tertium Quid principles, which must be brought to bear upon the political troubles of the present day. But even this state-ment of purpose seems a bit too modest for a novel which, if it does not seriously predict southern secession, is nonetheless anxious to claim a very bright future for the region. That was, after all, a risky prediction in 1836: Tucker was writing almost immediately after the Nullification dispute in South Carolina, a crisis that forced all south-erners to contemplate their diminished political power in the Union. In 1831 both Nat Turner's insurrection and the founding of Garrison's *Liberator* had occurred. Ten years earlier the Missouri crisis had seemed to close off a large part of the West to the institution of slavery. All these developments seemed to call the South's future into serious ques-tion. It was within this atmosphere of gloom that Tucker, trying imagi-natively to claim a brilliant future for his region, wrote his fantasy about an emerging southern nation.

He had, that is, at least two different purposes in writing his novel. He hoped to urge a return to the principles of the past, but he also wished to express a boundless confidence in the future; on one hand he wanted to declare his loyalty to the old Quid vision of a small, stable, pastoral republic, and on the other he could not resist imagin-ing, with giddy exhilaration, the emergence of a historically destined southern empire. The two purposes did not consist particularly well with each other, and his attempt to harmonize them led him to create a novel full of internal contradictions, which represented the confusion of the South itself in the years between the Missouri Compromise and the Civil War.

We might begin exploring these contradictions by returning to the

13. Quoted in Beverley D. Tucker, *Nathaniel Beverley Tucker: Prophet of the Con-federacy, 1784–1851* (Tokyo, 1979).

question with which we began—that of the setting. Van Buren is always situated in plush surroundings which suggest the corruption of "court"; the Virginia partisans live in a declining rural village, leading as best they can the lives of Jeffersonian yeomen. These two settings fit comfortably into the Tertium Quid view of the world: the moral implications of such a dichotomy are clear, and one may easily see why Tucker chose to invoke it in framing his republican critique of contemporary American politics. But a very large part of the novel, and indeed most of its significant action, takes place in neither of these settings but on Bernard Trevor's large plantation. It is there that Douglas receives the political education that turns him into a secessionist. Bernard is in a position to offer this education—he has been able to acquire his own expertise in political philosophy—because he is a wealthy planter, freed from the need to labor with his hands. It is at this plantation as well that the plot to liberate Virginia is unveiled by Bernard's friend Mr. ———, a mysterious intellectual who takes charge of the resistance. Indeed, through most of the book we move back and forth between Van Buren's office and Bernard's plantation, watching the antagonists maneuver against one another; and in most respects the real conflict of the novel—the conflict of ideas—is the one waged between these two symbolic realms.

It would not be accurate to say that the republican ideology was intrinsically opposed to the plantation; Taylor and Randolph, after all, were planters, as were dozens of other well-known republican statesmen. But the plantation did not serve particularly well as a symbol of the republic's virtue: that role was best filled by the self-sufficient small farm. Tucker, of course, knew this as well as anyone; thus once he begins to describe Virginia's struggle for the redemption of the republic, he prudently shifts the scene to his rural village in the piedmont. The heroes don homespun and even take assumed names (Douglas Trevor becoming "Captain Douglas") so as to conceal their membership in a rich planting family. They defer at appropriate moments to the homely wisdom of their social inferiors, particularly the resourceful scout Jacob Schwartz. And they fight in "the Indian way." But still we know that the principals of this struggle—Douglas, his brother Arthur, their cousin Delia—have nothing really to do with the log cabins in which they temporarily reside. Douglas and Delia—the hero and heroine whose marriage should seal the happy ending of the novel—will not be raising their children as barefoot rustics in the Blue Ridge foothills. They are products of the plantation, and it is to the plantation that they will return when the struggle for the pastoral republic is ended.

What are we to make of Tucker's attempt to conflate these two very different symbolic settings? Why complicate things by bringing the plantation into the otherwise simple Manichaean struggle between the deserted village and the corrupt city? It was not that the plantation had become the dominant institution in southern society; many historians have now documented the presence of a very large middle class in the antebellum South, including a considerable number of those yeoman farmers whose virtue and independence Tucker wants to borrow for his cause. But the South of the yeoman farmers was not Tucker's new emerging South. If the country were to achieve the fabulous power and prosperity he predicts for it in *The Partisan Leader*, it would do so because of its cotton and tobacco plantations, not its self-sufficient farms.

The profitability of those plantations, in reality and in the novel, depended, of course, on the institution of slavery. Tucker did not place slavery at the center of the sectional crisis; the real conflicts between North and South, he thought, were political and economic. But he did believe in the institution and in *The Partisan Leader* seeks to defend it, principally by way of one remarkable episode, which deserves close attention. About midway through the story, after Douglas and Bernard have foiled Van Buren's effort to control a local election, the two are charged with treason and a company of federal troops arrives at Bernard's plantation to arrest them. Bernard and B——, anticipating such a maneuver from the president, have taken the extraordinary precaution of arming the plantation slaves. When the troops arrive, these slaves—acting the part the Yankees expect of them, that of miserable chattels eager to be delivered from bondage—win their trust, then quickly produce their guns and take the soldiers captive.

Now the scene obviously partakes of a fair amount of wishful thinking: Tucker, writing five years after the Nat Turner rebellion, is obviously telling worried readers what they desperately want to hear about the loyalty of slaves. He may even have in mind the persistent story that loyal slaves bore arms and helped suppress the Turner uprising. But the implications of the scene not only go beyond this purpose, they plainly contradict it. "Regular soldiers prisoners to negroes!" exclaims the Yankee commander (212); it was an extraordinary notion in 1836 and an uncomfortable one, no doubt, for Tucker and many of his readers. It is not merely that the slaves outwit white troops, though that idea was doubtless troubling enough (and Tucker tries to minimize the trouble by assuring us that the slaves were guided in their stratagems by white masters). It is that they bear arms in defense of freedom, exactly like Douglas' partisans, indeed exactly like the virtuous militiamen throughout republican mythology. By doing so, they inevitably partake of the republican association of citizenship and political virtue with the ability to bear arms—an association most notably enshrined, of course, in the Second Amendment to the Constitution. And just as the myth requires, this slave militia defeats trained regulars and thus proves the superiority of "natural" cunning to parade-ground tactics: like Douglas' partisans, their way is the Indian way. As if to emphasize this odd analogy between Virginia patriots and Virginia slaves, Tucker throughout the novel characterizes the condition of southerners under the tyrannical Yankee president as "slavery": "Thank God! you are now a freeman," says Bernard, after his nephew resolves to resist Van Buren (168). Finally, the author, speaking through the apparently omniscient B——, makes the analogy explicit. Reassuring Douglas of the slaves' reliability, B—— explains that Negroes are like southerners: a naturally benevolent and selfless people, slow to anger and reluctant to rebel against even the most glaringly unjust treatment. The slave's loyalty to his master, he concludes, is as firm as the South's loyalty to the Union (205–206).

At this the reader may shake his head in amazement. Though Tucker declines to extend this analogy to its logical conclusion, we can hardly avoid doing so: for the southerners, despite their bottomless patience, finally *have* risen in revolt. Might not their slaves do the same and with even more justification? For all his desire to defend slavery, Tucker gives us no alternative but to believe that slaves possess in full measure both the will and the right to resist tyranny. The admission is fatal to his attempted defense of slavery.

Tucker certainly understood how dangerous an admission this was and how near he was to making it. He raised, imaginatively, a dilemma the South did eventually face in its actual struggle for independence, when in 1865 the beleaguered Confederacy, pressed by hard necessity, voted to admit black troops into its army. By that time the implications of such a decision were plain to many: Senator Howell Cobb of Georgia worried that "if negroes will make good soldiers, our whole theory of slavery is wrong"; and General Robert Toombs of the same state agreed that "the worst calamity that could befall us would be to gain our independence by the valor of our slaves."[14] And yet by 1865 it seemed doubtful that the South could gain independence without them. This dilemma was actually nothing new; the dire military necessity of 1865 only raised in vivid form an issue with which southern intellectuals had been wrestling since the 1830s. They had come to believe that slavery was such a solidly entrenched feature of southern culture that it must be incorporated into the regional ideology. In the winter of 1831–1832, in the Virginia legislature, southern antislavery partisans had lost the last serious debate over the abolition of slavery to take place in the antebellum South. Thereafter it was impossible for southern republicans to follow the procedure of their ancestors—men such as Jefferson, Taylor, St. George Tucker, and John Randolph—of treating slavery as a more or less incidental flaw in the South's otherwise spotless republican virtue. If the South was to remain a slaveholding republic, then slavery must somehow be harmonized with republicanism—must indeed be enlisted in defense of that beleaguered body of thought. Other southern apologists were attempting the same difficult maneuver in their political rhetoric, citing the allegedly analogous slaveholding republics of Greece and Rome or insisting that black slavery abetted the cause of republicanism by ensuring the equality of all whites.[15] Tucker tries to dramatize the convergence of slavery and re-

14. Shelby Foote, *The Civil War: Red River to Appomattox* (New York, 1974), 859–60.

15. On "proslavery republicanism" in the South, see Tise, *Proslavery*, 347–62.

publicanism in his account of the slaves' triumph over Van Buren's regulars: he tries to represent—in circumstances remarkably like those eventually faced by the Confederacy—the paradoxical notion of slavery as the guarantor of liberty. Doing so requires him to walk a tightrope, the same one the Confederacy had to risk in 1865; it requires him to acknowledge the importance of slaves to southern freedom while still denying their right to participate in that freedom. It is probably to Tucker's credit that in the end he falls off the tightrope—that his effort to adapt the Doctrines of '98 to the felt needs of the contemporary South leads him, despite his own conscious purposes, to expose the contradiction between republicanism and slavery.

The most unusual thing about *The Partisan Leader* is, of course, that its action takes place in the future. A bit of literary history may help us grasp how remarkable this is, for southern literature is usually thought of as a literature of memory. Southern writing generally, both before and after the Civil War, has tended to be retrospective and elegiac: Allen Tate's famous characterization of modern southern writing—"a literature conscious of the past in the present"—applies equally well to most earlier southern work.[16] *The Partisan Leader* is not a complete anomaly; there is a small but lively tradition of futuristic southern writing, a tradition carried forth by a handful of books contemporary with Tucker's and revived more recently by Walker Percy's comic dystopia, *Love in the Ruins*, and its sequel, *The Thanatos Syndrome*. But by and large the standard view of southern literature is accurate, and particularly as applied to the regional subgenre in which Tucker was working, that of the plantation novel.

The book normally considered the first plantation novel, George Tucker's *Valley of Shenandoah* (1824), is a melancholy account of the impoverishment and eventual destruction of a proud Virginia family. The Graysons are the very models of landed virtue: generous, independent, idealistic, valuing honor above all. These archaic virtues, as Tucker has it, finally unfit the family to survive in a world dominated by the (in the typology of the time) Yankee traits of energy, ambition, and greed. At the end of the novel, the Grayson daughter has been

16. Tate, "The New Provincialism," in *Collected Essays*, 292.

seduced and abandoned by a visiting Yankee, and her brother, seeking to right the wrong, is murdered by the scoundrel on the streets of New York City. Not even John Randolph could have mustered more gloom about the prospects of pastoral virtue in the modern world. The best-known plantation novel, John Pendleton Kennedy's *Swallow Barn*, is a much more cheerful work but in the end is no more hopeful about the prospects of the southern pastoral republic. The Virginia planters in the novel are the objects of gentle satire, the slavery issue lurks ominously in the background, and the whole work is animated by Kennedy's obvious desire to record a doomed way of life while it still may be observed. Given what we have seen about the intrinsic pessimism of the pastoral republican vision, its tendency to exalt the past and dread the future, the elegiac tone of these southern narratives seems natural. So does the southern writer's lingering affinity for the form of the historical romance, a form which, as George Dekker has argued, is principally concerned with the subjects of change and loss, with the distance between present and past.[17]

But Tucker, in *The Partisan Leader*, attempts a striking departure from this tradition. It is not merely that he sets his "historical" romance in the future. Nor is it merely that he projects a future full of bright prospects: that Douglas and Delia will apparently be united at last (though the author neglects to explain just how) and that Virginia will succeed in its war for independence. Once he has begun fantasizing about the prospects of a southern nation, Tucker is not to be satisfied by a mere happy ending: he seems to be projecting not just a victory over the Yankees but a virtual secular millennium. The South has escaped the corrupt Union and, having promptly lowered its tariff barriers, is enjoying fabulous prosperity, as are all the nations with which it trades. Virginia encounters its share of difficulties, but we are assured that in the end it will overcome them and take its rightful place at the head of this southern confederacy, there to reap at last the just rewards of its virtue. Not just the Trevor family, not just Virginia, but appar-

17. George Dekker, *The American Historical Romance* (Cambridge, Eng., 1987). Dekker argues that the "Waverly model" persisted in southern writing well into the twentieth century in works like Faulkner's *Absalom, Absalom!* and Tate's *The Fathers.*

ently all the world (save only the American North) is to be delivered
from trouble by the triumph of the southern confederacy. The prophecy
Tucker ends by offering is along the lines of South Carolinian Henry
Timrod's millennial vision in the 1861 secessionist poem "Ethnogenesis":

> . . . Could we climb
> Some mighty Alp, and view the coming time,
> The rapturous sight would fill
>   Our eyes with happy tears!
> Not only for the glories which a hundred years
> Shall bring us; not for lands from sea to sea,
> And wealth, and power, and peace, though these shall be:
> But for the distant peoples we shall bless,
> And the hushed murmurs of the world's distress: . . . .[18]

Timrod was anticipating (in the much-mocked phrase of Francis Fu-
kuyama) "the end of history," to be ushered in by a triumphant southern nation; and Tucker, at certain moments, seems to have his eye on
the same prospect.

But to predict such a utopian future for the region, whatever its
appeal to southern readers in 1836 (or 1861), would certainly have
puzzled the old Tertium Quids in whose name Tucker claimed to speak.
To John Taylor, who put his faith not in a secular millennium but in
the constant round of decay and regeneration, or to John Randolph,
who believed that the Virginia descendants of the founding fathers had
become so many ruffians, spitting tobacco juice while parsing the Constitution, the idea of the South's inevitable progress toward a golden
age would have been surprising indeed. "Change is not reform!" Randolph had warned the Virginia Constitutional Convention; indeed, for
him change was likely to be the opposite. The best hope offered by the
old pastoral republican doctrine was that of preserving, as long as possible, whatever relics of virtue had survived from a better past. What
Tucker attempted in his historical romance of the future was a complete reversal of this doctrine, a substitution of a millennial for an

---

18. Henry Timrod, "Ethnogenesis," in *The Collected Poems of Henry Timrod,* ed.
Edd Winfield Parks and Aileen Wells Parks (Athens, Ga., 1965), 94–95.

Edenic historical vision. Political virtue was to be achieved not by preserving the past but by anxiously pursuing the future.

Tucker's last and perhaps most remarkable revision of Old Republican principles is related to his progressivism. One of the author's most persistent mannerisms in the novel is that of comparing his heroes to the people he conceives to have been their literal and moral ancestors. These Virginians are, he says, "the descendants of the men who had defied Cromwell, in the plenitude of his power, and had cast off the yoke of George the Third, without waiting for the cooperation of the other colonies" (40). He accounts for the rebirth of Virginia's patriotism by claiming that "the spirit of John Randolph had risen from the sleep of death, and walked abroad through the scenes where his youthful shoulders had received the mantle of *his* eloquence from the hand of Henry" (40). By drawing these analogies, however, Tucker is not merely claiming that his fictional heroes are equal to these historical ones; by implication he asserts that they are superior. The ancestors fought bravely for sacred principles but in the end were frustrated: the English cavaliers lost their war, the Quids lost most of their battles, and even the revolutionary patriots created a nation that, despite its hopeful beginnings, has now lapsed into tyranny. Only the architects of southern nationhood have succeeded completely, winning a lasting victory. What it all amounts to is an ascending typology of republican heroism, the natural companion of the author's progressive historical vision.

Tucker emphasizes this hierarchy of republican heroism by sketching out a kind of synchronic representation of the same historical progression in his portraits of the novel's three main political spokesmen. Hugh Trevor is the good old Unionist who at last comes to see the error of this persuasion. Bernard Tucker, less successful and respected than Hugh in most callings, is in this matter his superior, having seen the necessity of rebellion much sooner. And even Bernard, before the novel is half over, has begun to defer routinely to the political wisdom of B——, a professional intellectual even further advanced in the mysteries of the secessionist faith. *The Partisan Leader* is fairly bursting with fantasy and wishful thinking, but the presentation of B—— may offer the most extreme example. By the midpoint of the novel B—— has taken complete charge of Virginia's secession movement, suavely directing the actions of heroic cavaliers; finally, Tucker awards this bookish fellow a military rank ("the colonel," everyone suddenly begins calling him) and has the putative hero Douglas Trevor unable to make a move without his guidance. If Hugh represents any number of old Virginia republicans, and if Bernard represents the prophetic Tertium Quid faction, John Randolph in particular, then B—— personifies what Tucker hoped would be the rise of a southern intellectual class dedicated to the job of interpreting their region to the world. Hugh Holman suggests, on fairly good circumstantial evidence, that B—— represents Beverley Tucker himself.[19] In any case, he certainly represents the intellectual class which Tucker tried his best to call into being, mainly so that he could claim membership in it. This trio represents both the progress of Virginia thought from revolutionary republicanism to secession and the simultaneous transfer of intellectual power from the hands of the planter-politicians to those of professional men of letters. It is hard to judge which transformation Tucker thought more desirable.

Nor is B—— the last stage of this progression. Above him stands the man who tells the story, Nathaniel Beverley Tucker himself. In his own age, Tucker was a lawyer and a judge, later a professor and perhaps a sort of prophet, but he never achieved the "hearing" he wished for himself, not even in the novel for which he expressed such high hopes. But in the millennial future he imagines here, he becomes the historian, the custodian of all Virginia's past: not just the revolution against northern tyranny but all the lesser events that predicted it. Just as John Randolph inherited "the mantle of his eloquence" from Patrick Henry, the author himself, by writing his novel, claims it from Randolph. Poor Beverley Tucker, struggling southern man of letters, becomes in his own fantasy the chosen spokesman of the pastoral republican vision.

Wish fulfillment no doubt has something to do with this element of Tucker's fantasy; as the descendant of two prominent Virginia families, Tucker was the heir to a political influence that largely eluded him throughout his life. But there is likely more to it than that. What

19. C. Hugh Holman, Introduction to *The Partisan Leader*, xxii.

he attempted in *The Partisan Leader* was to adapt the pastoral republican program to the needs of the present-day South, an enterprise that required considerable tinkering with the components of that program. His project could be accomplished only by a rethinking of basic concepts, followed by an effort to bring social reality into line with the new concepts. It was by its nature an intellectual endeavor: this new version of the regional identity could only be, in John Crowe Ransom's disapproving phrase, "poured in from the top." If the South were ever to become the nation Tucker wished it to be, it would require the forceful guidance of its intellectuals: that handful of "orators, statesmen and philosophers" whose influence John Randolph had disparaged. Tucker recognized this need early in his career; it was the impulse behind his founding of the Dardenne community, behind his decision to abandon elective politics in favor of literature, behind the composition of *The Partisan Leader*. In his presentation of B——, he does his best to make that necessity plain.

But even on the matter of the intellectual's claim to power, a matter surely close to his heart, Tucker seems to doubt his own vision. Consider the way his novel ends. B—— disappears from the last third of the story; once the partisan struggle is under way his place is taken by the rough scout Jacob Schwartz, who guides Douglas in his campaigns. And when, despite the best-laid plans of B——, Douglas finds himself in Van Buren's dungeon, his only chance for escape depends not on the brain trust behind him but again on Schwartz, who has followed Douglas and his captors directly into Washington City and—as resourceful there as in the wilderness—has put together a conspiracy for his rescue. One suspects that Tucker felt some lingering attachment to Randolph's republican teaching that the fate of the republic rested after all with "the people." But the people, left to their own devices, would never create the utopia Tucker has in mind.

Indeed, it seems that Tucker, for all his desire to imagine a southern millennium, feels in general the pull of the old, elegiac instincts. For he seems curiously unwilling or unable to imagine in any detail the happy ending of which he wants to assure us. When the novel ends, Douglas is Van Buren's prisoner; his father is about to suffer a similar fate; and Delia is evidently about to be delivered to her loathsome admirer, the younger Baker. Schwartz has launched his plot to liberate them, but the inside man in this scheme is none other than "the Prime Minister," who for reasons of his own wishes to move against Van Buren; no one could suppose that a country governed by the double of Oliver Dain would be an improvement over one ruled by Martin Van Buren. Evidently the contradictions involved in his attempt to adapt the republican ideology to the uses of an expanding, progressive slaveholding nation finally asserted themselves: in his inability to imagine any but a gloomy ending—more than in his endless disquisitions on the rights of the states—Tucker really became the disciple of John Randolph.

In the years after the publication of *The Partisan Leader*, Tucker's career seemed to confirm the bleak prophecy implied by the ending of the novel; he never achieved the standing he desired as a spokesman for southern nationhood and destiny. *The Partisan Leader* itself was a commercial and critical failure—"the prophecies of a vizored and crack-brained politician," one anonymous southern reviewer called it. The few publications that praised the book swam against a strong negative tide. When the Richmond *Messenger* ran a favorable notice some readers protested by canceling their subscriptions; among them—it is painful even to report it—was Tucker's brother Henry.[20] Unsurprisingly, Tucker gave up on his dream of fame and wealth as a romancer, though he was to write one more extended piece of fiction.[21] He did win some success as a scholar, publishing influential tracts on constitutional law and legal pleading. And he developed a reputation, at William and Mary and other Virginia colleges, as an inspiring speaker on the subject of southern patriotism: no student had ever left him, he boasted once, "without being, for the time, a Southern man in feeling and a State's rights man in conviction."[22] He acted the part of B—— at last, not in novels but at his lectern.

20. Brugger, *Beverley Tucker*, 133.
21. This was *Gertrude*, a love story set in Virginia and Washington, published serially in the *Southern Literary Messenger* in 1844.
22. Brugger, *Beverley Tucker*, 170.

At the age of sixty-six, near the end of his life, he tried once more to act that part on the national age; in 1850 he served as Virginia's delegate to the Nashville Convention, organized to discuss southern political problems in that year of crisis. The convention's deliberations carried no authority, and some regarded it as a waste of time; Tucker was able to attend only because Virginia's elected delegate had better things to do and sent the old man in his place. But he took his charge seriously: "My position is one for which I have long wished," he said; "my great fear is that I may disappoint expectations." [23] But as with so many of his other endeavors, he did end up disappointing at least his own expectations. He went to the convention in the hope of persuading his fellow southerners, as Bernard and B—— had persuaded Douglas Trevor, of the need for secession. But though all the delegates treated him with respect, he won support only from a handful of hotheaded South Carolinians. He returned home dispirited, soon fell ill, and died two months later. It was another ten years before his dream of southern nationhood came to fruition and, of course, only another five before—as its would-be prophet might have predicted—it came to ruin.

23. *Ibid.*, 185.

4

George Fitzhugh Among the Cannibals: Sociology and the South

In 1849 George Fitzhugh, a middle-aged and rather unsuccessful Virginia lawyer, published at his own expense a short pamphlet entitled *Slavery Justified, by a Southerner.* He had been moved to write it, he explained, because he had concluded "that slavery, *black or white*, was right and necessary." He claimed that by arguing thus he was merely expressing the general if usually inarticulate sentiment of the South; and yet he also claimed that his ideas were so original and radical that few editors would have the "stern courage and integrity" to publish them—thus the need to issue his tract privately. He was the first, he concluded, "to write the *Justification and Philosophy of Slavery.*"[1]

Perhaps the first thing to notice about these claims is that they were all probably false. Very few southerners were prepared to believe that slavery was an appropriate condition for non-Africans; yet the southern press had for years displayed an insatiable appetite for proslavery apologetics, however farfetched; and as for the originality of his effort, most of the arguments Fitzhugh made were long familiar to southerners and indeed had been developed originally by New Englanders 150 years earlier.[2]

The whole enterprise was odd: why did Fitzhugh—who had previously displayed no literary or philosophical ambitions and indeed very little ambition of any sort—undertake to defend slavery? Why, if he was determined to defend it, did he circulate his pamphlet only among

---

1. George Fitzhugh, *Slavery Justified,* included as an appendix in *Sociology for the South, or, The Failure of Free Society* (Richmond, 1854), 225.

2. As Larry Tise has argued in *Proslavery.*

friends, in the immediate vicinity of his home in Caroline County—why defend slavery to a society of slaveholders? And why, if again his purpose was to justify slavery, did he devote so much space to other subjects, principally to the diagnosis, in terms borrowed from Thomas Carlyle and Auguste Comte, of the general malaise of Western civilization? Finally, why the contradictory claims with which he introduced his tract—on one hand, of a complete union with the common mind of the South, and on the other, of a radical philosophical originality? Yet for all the oddity of his enterprise, there was something remarkable about the Whitmanian boldness with which Fitzhugh burst upon the scene, advertising himself shamelessly. A sufficiently alert observer, had there been one among the small readership of *Slavery Justified,* might have discerned in it the beginnings of one of the most remarkable careers in antebellum southern letters.

The general outline of Fitzhugh's teaching has become familiar to students of American thought, to whom he has come to seem an irresistibly interesting eccentric. He was probably the most abstract, the most determinedly philosophical, of the proslavery intellectuals who emerged in the South between 1830 and 1860—a group that also included George Frederick Holmes, Albert Taylor Bledsoe, James Henry Hammond, Henry Hughes, and others. Unlike many previous southern apologists for the peculiar institution, Fitzhugh was not content simply to insist that slavery, whatever its flaws, could hardly be abolished overnight; or to maintain that it was a usually humane system which, by "civilizing" Africans and introducing them to Christianity, was doing them more good than harm; or even to suggest that it offered the most appropriate social role for Africans, who were for various reasons unfit for freedom. He went further, attacking not merely freedom for African Americans but freedom itself. He performed, as C. Vann Woodward has said, "a Nietzschean transvaluation of values," rejecting what had heretofore been the unchallengeable ultimate terms of American political discourse—freedom and democracy—and openly praising their opposites, slavery and aristocracy.[3]

---

3. C. Vann Woodward, "George Fitzhugh, *Sui Generis,*" Introduction to George Fitzhugh, *Cannibals All! or, Slaves Without Masters* (Cambridge, Mass., 1960), xxi.

Because of his flamboyant contrariness, Fitzhugh has become a figure of fascination to students of American thought. Many scholars have taken him as a personification of the South's departure from its liberal heritage, not to mention its senses, under the pressure of abolitionist criticism after 1830. A bit more unconventional has been the response of Woodward and Louis Hartz, liberals who—concerned about the danger of liberal complacency—have deplored Fitzhugh's teachings but valued him as a disturber of the peace, a rare antiliberal voice amid the dreary "consensus" of American politics. Even more unconventionally, the self-styled "Marxist conservative" Eugene Genovese has admitted an unstinting admiration for Fitzhugh ("I have come to think of him as an old friend"), whom he regards as the author of a proto-Marxist critique of liberal capitalism and the voice of a genuinely pre-bourgeois, communal social vision.[4]

Fitzhugh was likewise a figure of fascination to at least a few of his own contemporaries. Among the southerners to whom his books were addressed, a handful of critics greeted them with a somewhat puzzled appreciation, while the great majority simply ignored them.[5] But he was taken up with great enthusiasm by his enemies in the North. William Lloyd Garrison was delighted to cite Fitzhugh's most provocative statements as typical of the madness of the South, and Abraham Lincoln borrowed one of his most famous observations—that the country could not endure half-slave and half-free—from Fitzhugh. In at least one way Fitzhugh deserved the attention of these northern foes of

4. Louis Hartz, *The Liberal Tradition in America: An Interpretation of American Political Thought Since the Revolution* (New York, 1955); Eugene D. Genovese, *The World the Slaveholders Made: Two Essays in Interpretation* (New York, 1969), 119.

5. Typical of the puzzled admirers was G. C. Grammer, who reviewed *Sociology for the South* in *De Bow's Review*, XIX (1855), 29–38. Grammer found that the book "would afford an hour's most delightful reading to the dullest man in christendom" (this was meant as praise) but warned that many of the author's most extreme statements must be taken "*cum grano salis.*" Fitzhugh's most enthusiastic praise came from his friend George Frederick Holmes, an English-born professor of philosophy at the University of Virginia, who contrived to review *Sociology for the South* twice, in the *Southern Literary Messenger*, XXI (March, 1855), 129–41, and the *Quarterly Review of the Methodist Episcopal Church, South*, IX (April, 1855), 180–201.

slavery, for he was essentially the only southern apologist prepared to answer the question inevitably raised by the "positive good" argument for slavery: if the institution was such a benevolent one, why did the South wish to limit its benefits to Africans only? We don't, he calmly replied in behalf of his region—or at least we shouldn't. To be sure, most Africans were fit only for slavery, but so were most people of all races. "We deem this peculiar question of Negro slavery of very little importance," he said. "The issue is made throughout the world on the general subject of slavery in the abstract."[6]

To state his most extreme conclusions so baldly is to risk caricaturing Fitzhugh and thus obscuring the force that his writing sometimes achieves. For he was nothing if not a shrewd and able propagandist, equipped with a flair for rhetoric and a debater's instinct for the jugular. Consider for instance his second book, *Cannibals All!* (1859), which may be his most effective polemic. The meaning of his title was that cannibalism—the violent exploitation of man by man—was the nature of life in free society. "You are a Cannibal," he advises the northern capitalist, "and if a successful one, pride yourself on the number of your victims, quite as much as any Fiji chieftain, who breakfasts, dines, and sups on human flesh."[7] To contemplate the cultural resonances this charge must have set off in the American nineteenth century is to see something of Fitzhugh's canniness as an advocate. For cannibalism was an oddly persistent theme in American writing during this period; one thinks of William Prescott's Aztecs in *The Conquest of Mexico*, Francis Parkman's Iroquois in *France and England in North America*, and above all Herman Melville's Polynesians in *Typee* and *Moby-Dick*. For Prescott and Parkman, as David Levin has argued, cannibalism worked as a symbol of savagery and also of a perverse brand of civilization: a morbidly refined cruelty that was both the opposite and the natural companion of savagery. Both were to be distinguished from the healthy,

---

6. Lincoln, however, did not know the source. The statement appeared in 1856 in an unsigned editorial in the Richmond *Enquirer*, a paper to which Lincoln subscribed, and he mistakenly attributed it to the *Enquirer*'s editor, Roger Pryor. See Harvey Wish, *George Fitzhugh, Propagandist of the Old South* (Baton Rouge, 1943), 150. The quotation is from Fitzhugh, *Sociology*, 95.

7. Fitzhugh, *Cannibals All!*, 17.

progressive, natural vigor of European and particularly of Anglo-Saxon institutions. The legend of European Protestant destiny—what Herbert Butterfield termed "the Whig interpretation of history"—was among other things the legend of the defeat of cannibalism by liberal institutions.[8] It was into this intellectual milieu—in a nation beginning to believe in its "Manifest Destiny," its own particular chapter in the Whig historical vision—that Fitzhugh came forward to announce that American "free society," the very flowering of Anglo-Saxon liberalism, was as cannibalistic as the Fiji Islands. In doing so he displayed an instinct for cultural pressure points not much less shrewd than Melville's, whose portrayal of Queequeg similarly upends conventional assumptions about the moral superiority of American liberal culture: "We cannibals must help these Christians," thinks the admirable harpooner. Fitzhugh knew how to make an argument.

And yet, for all his ability as a partisan, he cannot help seeming to us, as he did to many of his contemporaries, more than a little eccentric. He certainly followed his own injunction to ignore immediate historical circumstances and make his case "in the abstract." Thus in the middle of the Civil War—on the eve, as it happened, of the Battle of Gettysburg—Fitzhugh offered his final analysis of the sectional conflict. While others spoke of the indissoluble Union or the rights of the states, of the claims of slaves or of slaveholders, he calmly announced that southerners—including presumably the butternut troops then poised at the foot of Cemetery Ridge—were engaged in "a solemn protest against the doctrines of natural liberty, human equality, and the social contract," indeed an "attempt to roll back the Reformation in its political phases."[9]

This information would have come as a surprise, no doubt, to the troops themselves—to those infamously profane, anarchic Confederates whose fierce individualism made them such formidable fighters

---

8. David Levin, *History as Romantic Art: Bancroft, Prescott, Motley, and Parkman* (Stanford, 1959); Herbert Butterfield, *The Whig Interpretation of History* (New York, 1965).

9. George Fitzhugh, "The Revolutions of 1776 and 1861 Contrasted," *Southern Literary Messenger*, XXXV (1863), 722–23. Hartz dates the composition of the piece at the time of the Gettysburg campaign; see *Liberal Tradition*, 145.

and indifferent soldiers. It would have come as a considerable surprise, in fact, to most southerners—a people so jealous of personal and local liberties that their fledgling nation, as David Donald has said, "died of democracy."[10] But Fitzhugh never backed away from this or any other of his extreme formulations. It strikes me that the most significant thing about him, taken as a representative of the antebellum southern intellectual, was probably not his wrongness on these matters—many Americans, North and South, managed to be equally wrong. What makes Fitzhugh interesting, representative, and in some respects even sympathetic, was his perverse lifelong refusal to admit any error, his stubborn adherence to his eccentric notions in the face of the over-whelmingly contrary evidence around him.

The boldness Fitzhugh displayed in 1849, when he announced his discovery of "the justification and philosophy of slavery," never deserted him. And he was in at least one respect as original as he claimed to be: though the impulse to defend slavery as "a positive good" had moved many southerners before him, Fitzhugh was among the first to supplement these defenses—which he dismissed as "excuses, apologies, and palliations"—with a spirited counterattack on the dominant social habits of the North. "For thirty years," he said, "the South has been a field on which abolitionists, foreign and domestic, have carried on offensive warfare. Let us now, in turn, act on the offensive, transfer the seat of war, and invade the enemy's territory."[11] His idea of the South thus depended absolutely on his countervailing idea of the North. Accordingly, the best place to begin understanding Fitzhugh's effort to distill the southern identity is with his attack on the rival region, the photographic negative by which he defined his positive image.

What did the North represent for Fitzhugh? The principal theme of his attack on the region, expressed in his two major tracts, *Sociology for the South* (1854) and *Cannibals All!* (1859), was the practical and

---

10. David Donald, "Died of Democracy," in *Why the North Won the Civil War*, ed. Donald (Baton Rouge, 1960).

11. Fitzhugh, *Sociology*, 222.

moral failure of "free society." By this term he meant the culture of liberal capitalism as projected by John Locke and Adam Smith, a culture which he believed dominated social and economic life in the North and much of Europe. Fitzhugh began attacking the errors of free society at what he considered their origin, the social contract theory proposed in Locke's *Treatises of Government.* "We believe," he said, "no theory in moral science has been more pregnant of mischief than this theory of Locke." There had been no "state of nature" in which man was free, he insisted, thus no "contract" in which he voluntarily surrendered his freedom. Man was intrinsically a social being, was indeed the product of society; therefore, "he has no rights whatever, as opposed to the interests of society." Indeed, the very term *free society* was oxymoronic, since the liberal ethos of individualism could produce no genuine community but only "dissociation of labor and disintegration of society." [12]

The leading doctrine of free society, he said, "and almost its only doctrine, is that individual well-being and social and national well-being and prosperity will be best promoted by each man's eagerly pursuing his own selfish welfare, unfettered and unrestricted by legal restrictions or governmental prohibitions, farther than such regulations may be necessary to prevent positive crime." This doctrine, Fitzhugh believed, engendered "war in the bosom of society," and because it declined to acknowledge that the war was waged on unequal terms, by people of unequal abilities, it inevitably permitted the exploitation of the weak by the strong. In free society all were "cannibals," doing their best to exploit their fellows. The strongest became in effect "masters," but their power was accompanied by no responsibility for those they commanded. The weakest were for practical purposes slaves, but "slaves without masters," which was to say without any guarantee of security or even of subsistence. Because of the injustice of this arrangement, which had created in Europe and the North a mass of desperate and dispossessed laborers, "free society" in those regions was in chaos, beset by poverty, crime, and revolution: "The ink was hardly dry with which Adam Smith wrote his *Wealth of Nations*, lauding the benign influences

12. *Ibid.*, 25, 27.

of free society, ere the hunger and want and nakedness of that society engendered a revolutionary explosion that shook the world to its
centre. The starving artisans and laborers and fish women and needle
women of Paris, were the authors of the first French revolution, and
that revolution was everywhere welcomed and spread from nation to
nation like a fire in the prairies." Though the North had so far escaped
the danger of massive revolution, the failure of its free society could
be inferred, Fitzhugh thought, from the proliferation of reform movements there. Why, he asked the North rhetorically, "have you Bloom-
ers and Women's Rights men, and strong-minded women, and Mor-
mons, and anti-renters, and 'vote myself a farm' men, Millerites, and
Spiritual Rappers, and Shakers, and Widow Wakemanites, and Agrarians, and Grahamites, and a thousand other superstitious and infidel
-isms at the North? Why is there faith in nothing, speculation about
everything? Why is this unsettled, half-demented state of the human
mind coextensive in time and space, with free society?" [13]

What was Fitzhugh's purpose in thus attacking northern freedom?
The defense of slavery, no doubt; but anyone who has read Fitzhugh's
tracts is aware of their tendency to wander far from their ostensible
subject and to explore at length, to no apparent purpose, whatever
social questions have attracted the author's vagrant attention. And
those tracts had scant circulation outside the South; they were aimed
primarily at an audience already convinced of the goodness, or at least
the inevitability, of slavery. Thus the ostensible purpose of his exertions

---

13. *Ibid.*, 49, 22, 39–40, 103. The final passage recalls a similar catalog of "infidel
-isms" reported by a more sympathetic but nonetheless amused observer of New England idealism; Ralph Waldo Emerson is describing the convention of the Friends of
Universal Reform, sponsored by William Lloyd Garrison and held in Chardon Street
Chapel in Boston in November, 1840: "If the assembly was disorderly, it was pictur-
esque. Madmen, madwomen, men with beards, Dunkers, Muggletonians, Come-outers,
Groaners, Agrarians, Seventh-day Baptists, Quakers, Abolitionists, Calvinists, Unitari-
ans and Philosophers—all came successively to the top, and seized their moment, if
not their hour, wherein to chide, or pray, or protest. Their faces were a study. The
most daring innovators and the champions-until-death of the old causes sat side by
side" ("The Chardon Street Convention," in *Lectures and Biographical Sketches* [Boston,
1911], 374–75, Vol. X of Emerson, *Complete Works*, 12 vols.).

seems not fully to account for them. I suspect that for Fitzhugh a large part of the importance of the slavery issue was that it afforded him a highly visible pulpit from which to expound his philosophy. His books were principally meant as exercises in social prescription, performed (as the title *Sociology for the South* would imply) for the edification of his region.

How, then, did his denunciations of the North fit into these exercises in social philosophy? It seems clear that "South" and "North" functioned for him, as they did for John Taylor and John Randolph, as the symbols of certain social goods and evils. For all the gleeful malice in some of his antinorthern diatribes, he does not seem to have harbored much real sectional prejudice. He was openly impressed by the orderly prosperity of the New England towns he saw on his one visit to the North. He freely acknowledged the region's superior material and cultural wealth. And he spoke respectfully of northern abolitionists, including his friend and distant kinsman Gerrit Smith. He meant something more complicated than a regional insult when he flung his bewildering array of charges at free society in the North: social dislocation, economic predation, religious heresy, and reformism run amok. What did these errors have in common? What, specifically, did northern free society represent in Fitzhugh's system of moral geography?

Our first clue may be found in one of the strangest aspects of Fitzhugh's indictment of the North: his tendency to associate that region—linked to commerce and industry since the appearance of Alexander Hamilton's "Report on Manufactures" in 1791—with western Europe, a society in the grip of radical revolution since the fall of the Bastille in 1789. One may readily see why such a conservative as Fitzhugh viewed with alarm the spirit of revolution which, when he wrote his first tract in 1849, had once again swept across the Continent. But what was it about the capitalist North that linked it with that force—what has Babbitt in common with Robespierre? The critic Donald Pease offers a hint by arguing that the basic social ethos of Jacksonian America was "revolutionary." By this he means that the national tradition—based, after all, on a revolution—included the imperative of ceaseless change. One could best honor the founders of the country by following their example: one must begin each day, as it were, by resolving to forget yesterday. Marvin Meyers has similarly characterized the age as one of abrupt social, economic, and political change—change which Americans both feared and desired, a contradictory attitude that found expression in the conservative-progressive rhetoric of Andrew Jackson.[14] Both Meyers and Pease are, of course, following the lead of George Fitzhugh's contemporary and fellow critic of democracy Alexis de Tocqueville. The author of *Democracy in America*, who had seen firsthand the effects of the revolutionary ethos in western Europe, found similarly revolutionary tendencies even in the comparatively peaceful democracy of the United States: "Among democratic nations," he said,

> new families are constantly springing up, others are constantly falling away, and all that remain change their condition; the woof of time is every instant broken and the track of generations effaced. Those who went before are soon forgotten; of those who will come after, no one has any idea; the interest of man is confined to those in close propinquity to himself. As each class approximates to other classes, and intermingles with them, its members become indifferent and as strangers to one another. . . . Thus not only does democracy make every man forget his ancestors, but it hides his descendants and separates his contemporaries from him; it throws him back forever upon himself alone and threatens in the end to confine him entirely to the solitude of his own heart.[15]

The essential turbulence Tocqueville noted in antebellum America can be attributed to a variety of causes. It was the age of Jacksonian democracy, when political power was abruptly distributed much more widely than ever before. It was also an age when an old-fashioned agrarian economy, in which most manufacturing was at the level of handcraft and much exchange still at the level of barter, was being transformed into a capitalist marketplace. Andrew Jackson spoke for many when he charged that this marketplace (symbolized by the Bank of the United States) was subject to "great and sudden fluctuations . . .

14. Donald Pease, *Visionary Compacts* (Madison, Wisc., 1985); Marvin Meyers, *The Jacksonian Persuasion: Politics and Belief* (2nd ed.; Stanford, 1960).

15. Alexis de Tocqueville, *Democracy in America*, trans. Henry Reeve (New York, 1947), 312.

rendering property insecure and the wages of labor unsteady and un-
certain." It was an age of western expansion, when the old American
republic began to imagine itself as a continental empire. Nor should
we overlook what George Forgie has taught us about the peculiar psy-
chic pressures of this moment in the nation's history—the moment
when the generation that had made the American Revolution were
dying out. "One great link, connecting us with former times, was broken," said Daniel Webster about the nearly simultaneous deaths of
Jefferson and Adams on July 4, 1826; thus Americans "were driven on,
by another great remove from the days of the country's early distinction, to meet posterity and to vie with the future."[16] Six years later
Charles Carroll, the last living signer of the Declaration of Independence, also died, and the "sons" of these heroes suddenly found themselves uncomfortably alone in possession of the republic. All these
circumstances combined to create a general fear that flux had become
the rule in American life, that no still point remained to cling to.

Fitzhugh shared the alarm, voiced by Tocqueville and many others,
about the threat of uncontrolled change in America. And having recognized a destructive force abroad in the land, he followed an old
southern custom by identifying it with the North. It was this tendency
that united all the apparently diverse characteristics he attributed to
the rival region: social dislocation, economic predation, religious heresy, and a passion for anything calling itself reform. And it was this
which likened the tame, capitalist North to violent, revolutionary
Europe.

And what of the South? What did it represent in Fitzhugh's system
of moral geography? We might begin by distinguishing that system from
those of his southern republican predecessors. For Taylor and Randolph, as we have seen, the South represented an archaic, pastoral,
and republican virtue; the North represented commerce, power, and
corruption, the enemies of such virtue. By defending the South the
Old Republicans hoped to preserve, locally, an image of the social ideal

16. Jackson quoted in Michael T. Gilmore, *American Romanticism and the Marketplace* (Chicago, 1985), 21; Forgie, *Patricide in the House Divided;* Daniel Webster, "Adams and Jefferson," in *The Works of Daniel Webster* (6 vols.; Boston, 1853), I, 114.

toward which all America ought to aspire. Now Fitzhugh certainly granted that the South was more nearly pastoral than the North, but he regretted the fact profoundly. He insisted that "a single family, man, wife, and two or three children, under twenty-one years of age, cannot carry on farming profitably." The yeoman farmer was doomed to destitution and debt, the reverse of virtuous independence. As for the South as a whole, the agrarian region which Taylor thought might save the republic, Fitzhugh believed that its exclusive devotion to agriculture had impoverished it culturally and economically: he likened it to Ireland and the East and West Indies, "poor and ignorant countries with rich soils." Taylor had, of course, feared the decline of agriculture and the yeoman's loss of his land—the perennial nightmares of the pastoral imagination—and had hoped that these disasters might be prevented by scientific agriculture. But Fitzhugh dismisses this remedy abruptly, noting that "the great secrets of animal and vegetable life . . . are in a great measure hidden from human search" and that farming was therefore "the proper pursuit of dull men." In an 1859 essay on the history of the Rappahannock River valley, Fitzhugh pays tribute to the master of Hazelwood but largely ignores his achievements in agriculture and political thought: Fitzhugh's Taylor was simply a planter who treated his slaves well. The South, Fitzhugh believed, must abandon its exclusive devotion to agriculture and develop an extensive manufacturing capacity, thus becoming more like Holland and (of all places) Massachusetts, "two of the richest, happiest, and most civilized states in the world, because they farm very little, and are engaged in more profitable and enlightened pursuits."[17]

Taylor's system had depended absolutely on his faith in the institution of private property—the notion of a natural and secure bond between the individual and his land. Fitzhugh acknowledged the persistence of this republican idea in his region, but again he accounted it a weakness and set about correcting it in his tracts. With his usual sure instinct for the cornerstone of an intellectual edifice, he began his

17. Fitzhugh, "Southern Thought," 297; Fitzhugh, *Sociology*, 156–57; George Fitzhugh, "The Valleys of Virginia—The Rappahannock," *De Bow's Review*, XXVI (1859), 279.

attack on the concept of property rights at its origin: the Lockean notion of the individual's inalienable property in himself. This property was certainly not inalienable, he thought, since history showed plainly that it *had* been alienated frequently in all times and places: life and liberty, he said, "have been sold in all countries, and in all ages, and must be sold as long as human nature lasts." In fact, the individual had no property in himself at all, for "society is the being—[the individual] one of the members of that being": each person, that is, belonged ultimately to the community, not to himself.[18] It followed that no other property was secure either. The Old Republicans had believed, as Pocock puts it, in a personality "founded in property." But Fitzhugh's southerner would have to anchor his being elsewhere, for property, in the sense familiar to John Taylor, was an illusion: it had no real existence.

For Taylor and other Old Republicans, the ultimate security of the pastoral republic lay not in land or in political ideas but in the "virtue" of the citizens, that is, in their determination to maintain personal and local liberty against the self-aggrandizing tendencies of government. Again Fitzhugh was prepared to acknowledge the persistence of this antique notion among his fellow southerners. But he was particularly concerned to rid the South of this infatuation, a relic of revolutionary days and a distinct liability for a society preparing to instruct the Western world in the utopian virtues of slavery. Thus "as civilization advances, liberty recedes," he said, "and it is fortunate for man that he loses his love of liberty just as fast as he becomes more moral and intellectual." The Old Republicans had held stubbornly to the Jeffersonian teaching about the government which governs least; but for Fitzhugh, "the best governed countries . . . have always been distinguished for the number and stringency of their laws." Indeed, in his rejection of the idea of independence Fitzhugh rejected, with remarkable succinctness, the entire venerable tradition of Anglo-American republicanism. He knew, of course, the famous words of Jefferson, written at the end of his life and the fiftieth anniversary of the signing of the Declaration of Independence: "The mass of mankind has not

18. Fitzhugh, *Sociology*, 179, 25.

been born with saddles on their backs, nor a favored few booted and spurred, ready to ride them legitimately, by the grace of God." He knew as well that Jefferson was echoing the last words, uttered on the gallows, of the English republican martyr Richard Rumbold, plotter against Charles II: "I am sure there was no Man born marked of God above another; for none comes into the World with a Saddle on his Back, neither any Booted and Spurr'd to Ride him." It was with both quotations in mind and the republican tradition they bracketed as well that Fitzhugh announced in *Sociology for the South* that "men are not born entitled to equal rights! It would be far nearer the truth to say 'that some were born with saddles on their backs, and others booted and spurred to ride them,'—and the riding does them good." Did men have no "inalienable rights" at all, then? Fitzhugh was prepared for the question: "About nineteen out of every twenty individuals," he said, "have 'a natural and inalienable right' to be taken care of and protected, to have guardians, trustees, husbands, or masters; in other words, they have a natural and inalienable right to be slaves."[19]

With so much said, Fitzhugh undoubtedly believed that he had effectively exorcised the old tradition of pastoral republicanism from his thought and begun the necessary task of forging a new southern identity. Certainly that was what he wished to do. And yet it was not quite so. Fitzhugh's thought may be the strongest testimonial of the remarkable persistence of the pastoral republican persuasion in the South, for that tradition had a way of reappearing, a kind of Banquo's ghost, at inopportune moments in his discourse. In the end, Fitzhugh's image of the South was fundamentally (though only fundamentally) similar to that of his predecessors.

"There must be a new world," said Thomas Carlyle in 1850, "or there will be no world at all."[20] Carlyle was the single greatest intel-

---

19. *Ibid.*, 30, 179; Jefferson, "Letter to Roger C. Weightman," June 24, 1826, in *Writings*, 1517; Richard Rumbold quoted in Douglass Adair, "Rumbold's Dying Speech, 1685, and Jefferson's Last Words on Democracy, 1826," in *Fame and the Founding Fathers: Essays by Douglass Adair*, ed. H. Trevor Colbourn (New York, 1974), 200; Fitzhugh, *Cannibals All!*, 69.

20. Thomas Carlyle, "The Present Time," in *Latter-Day Pamphlets* (New York, 1901), 1.

lectual influence on Fitzhugh. The Virginian fully agreed with his hero's diagnosis of the modern malaise and attempted to respond to it in forming his image of a redeemed and redemptive southern order. But he claimed that in offering the South for this redemptive task, he was offering not a new world but an old one.

To be sure, Fitzhugh often indulged his taste for paradox by suggesting that the reactionary South was actually the realization of the utopian daydreams of Yankee reformers. "Slavery is a form, and the very best form, of socialism," he said, and "a well-conducted farm in the South is a model of associated labor that Fourier might envy." "Towards slavery," he gloated, "the North and all Western Europe are unconsciously marching." Because it alone had solved the dilemma of free society, the American South was the most socially advanced country in the world, "about to lead the thought and direct the practices of christendom."[21]

And yet for all its supposed affinities with modern reform movements, Fitzhugh believed that southern slavery was best understood as a modern version of the communal, feudal, patriarchal order celebrated by Locke's dialectical opponent, the Tory philosopher Sir Robert Filmer, in his *Patriarcha*. Under slavery as under feudalism, Fitzhugh argued, there was a genuine community of interest between capital and labor. The master was compelled to assume responsibility for the well-being of his laborer, who was thus guaranteed the security denied him by free society. The relationship between master and slave was founded on personal responsibility, not merely the cash nexus; a slave society, therefore, fostered community, whereas free society encouraged only selfishness and rampant individualism. "It is domestic slavery alone," he said, "that can establish a safe, efficient and human community of property. It did so in ancient times, it did so in feudal times, and does so now, in Eastern Europe, Asia and America. Slaves never die of hunger; seldom suffer want. . . . A Southern farm is a sort of joint stock concern, or social phalanstery, in which the master furnishes the capital and skill, and the slaves the labor, and divide the profits, not according to each one's in-put, but according to each one's wants and

21. Fitzhugh, *Sociology*, 27, 45; Fitzhugh, "Southern Thought," 275.

necessities." It was for this reason, he concluded, that while Europe and the North were in turmoil, "at the slaveholding South, all is peace, quiet, plenty and contentment. We have no mobs, no trades unions, no strikes for higher wages, no armed resistance to the law, but little jealousy of the rich by the poor. We have but few in our jails, and fewer in our poor houses."[22] Southern slavery, then, was simultaneously radical and conservative, innovative and ancient, the one reform that would obviate the need of others: the "-ism," one might say, to end "-isms."

The South, that is, represented permanence to Fitzhugh, as the North represented change. It is this fundamental aspect of his analysis which finally betrays Fitzhugh's kinship with the Old Republicans he gleefully rejected. Like Taylor and Randolph and the rest, Fitzhugh's imagination was haunted by the fear of chaos and flux, by the threat of dispossession. One is not surprised to learn that *The Deserted Village* was among his favorite works of literature; it contained, he believed, more social truth than any work of political economy, and its author was second only to Shakespeare among English poets.[23] For the threat Fitzhugh believed his country was facing was precisely the one recorded in Goldsmith's influential poem—the destruction of a virtuous community, brought about by external forces of radical change. And like many of his Virginia ancestors, he made it his project to locate some still point immune to such change—and to locate it, ideally, in the South. For them the foundations of permanence had been agricultural life, secure personal property, and political independence: the cluster of ideas that made up the pastoral republican ideology. But Fitzhugh systematically rejected the components of that ideology, not because they were intrinsically contemptible but because they were, he believed, impermanent. His work, it seems to me, must be understood as an attempt to learn, amid the flux of American social life, just what *was* permanent.

It is in this context that all of Fitzhugh's eccentric claims about southern slavery begin to assemble themselves into a coherent state-

22. Fitzhugh, *Sociology*, 47–48, 233.
23. Wish, *George Fitzhugh*, 259–60.

ment. Slavery, he said, was an ancient, almost prehistoric institution, far older in world-historical terms than republicanism. Even in the limited span of Virginia history (as he argued in his important 1859 essay "The Valleys of Virginia—The Rappahannock") republicanism was a late arrival; the original institutions of Virginia were slavery and aristocracy; in 1680, he boasted, even white immigrants to Virginia "were considered as 'goods, wares and merchandise,' to be sold publicly at places appointed by law." But slavery was also a progressive institution, destined to dominate the future. And slavery was universal, life and liberty having been sold in all countries and ages throughout history. Nor was slavery, properly considered, a racial institution—the "peculiar question of Negro slavery" was of very little importance, the real issue being "slavery in the abstract." Southern slavery, in other words, was anything but what John Calhoun had called it, a "peculiar institution." The burden of Fitzhugh's proslavery writing is to disentangle American slavery from all its local particularities of nationality, region, and race, the incidental residue of time and place, and reveal it as a timeless essence: that is, to wrench it out of history and make it instead a part of nature. Thus the slave trade, as Fitzhugh argued in *De Bow's Review* in 1857, was "as old, as natural, and irresistible as the tides of the ocean."[24]

Fitzhugh was determined to claim for slavery, that is, exactly what the pastoral, and pastoral republican politics, had claimed for agrarian life: that it was ancient, natural, and stable. Slavery conferred what every pastoral figure since Virgil's Tityrus has longed for, inalienable claims—for instance, "the inalienable right to be slaves." Slavery is the genuinely permanent institution, outside of history and thus immune to destructive change. In Fitzhugh's bizarre inversion of Virginia thought, slavery becomes not a threat to the pastoral dream but its ultimate fulfillment.

This is the conclusion toward which Fitzhugh's arguments have been driving us. Agricultural life must be rejected: agricultural states were invariably exploited and eventually destroyed by industrial ones. Likewise, the idea of property: upon analysis it too proved to be a structure

24. Fitzhugh, "Valleys," 281; final quotation from Wish, *George Fitzhugh,* 241.

built on sand, doomed by its own internal logic. And likewise independence itself: a free country, he believed, was ineluctably headed for political, economic, and social chaos; the citizens of such a country, finally oppressed beyond endurance by the terrible consequences of freedom, would at length demand a benevolent tyranny—would assert their "natural and inalienable right to be slaves." Agriculture, property, liberty—all were noble-sounding notions built on weak foundations: they would not endure. What would? What institution was sufficiently permanent to fulfill the pastoral daydream of permanence? Slavery was, he decided at last.

Thus did Fitzhugh solve the great problem of social flux in nineteenth-century America. Contemplating an America enamored of chaotic, bustling, pointless movement, he offered the South as an image of a better world: a South characterized, he claimed, by peace and harmony, by freedom from economic predation and marketplace values, by a hierarchical social order supervised by benevolent aristocrats, to whom lesser folk, black and white, gratefully deferred. Few will be surprised to discover that a great deal of scholarship on the Old South tends to dispute Fitzhugh's claims. Since Frank Owsley published his classic *Plain Folk of the Old South* in 1949, many historians, though departing from Owsley on important questions, have followed him in developing a convincing portrait of white southerners as largely middle class in status and outlook: as devoted to progress, equality, and democracy and as little inclined to defer to an aristocratic "master class," as anyone else in Andrew Jackson's America.[25] And Fitzhugh himself, I shall argue, was almost certainly well acquainted with these southerners. When he painted his portrait of a feudal South, he was responding to complicated motives, among which a devotion to careful empiricism ranked comparatively low.

25. Frank L. Owsley, *Plain Folk of the Old South*, Introduction by Grady McWhiney (1949; rpr. Baton Rouge, 1982); see also J. Mills Thornton III, *Politics and Power in a Slave Society: Alabama, 1800–1860* (Baton Rouge, 1978); James Oakes, *The Ruling Race: A History of American Slaveholders* (New York, 1982); and Cooper, *Liberty and Slavery*.

It will help to get an idea of what exactly Fitzhugh was forced to ignore about his region to arrive at his findings. It helps to notice, for instance, that while Fitzhugh was insisting that "we of the South . . . have been 'calm as a summer's evening,' quite unconscious of the storm brewing around us," his fellow southerners were killing and maiming each other at such a frantic pace as to make their region, according to the historian Dickson Bruce, the most violent part of the country in the nineteenth century, excepting only the far western frontier. This assertion Bruce supports with an impressive catalog of southern mayhem, ranging from the duels of gentlemen to the stomp-and-gouge contests of plain folk. Kenneth Greenberg has gone so far as to argue that Congressman Preston Brooks, at the moment he brutally caned Charles Sumner on the floor of the Senate, achieved a nearly perfect symbolization of southern culture—a judgment many admiring southerners were glad to affirm at the time.[26]

Fitzhugh's South had achieved its peace and harmony by virtue of being an aristocratic society: slave-owning planters wielded all the power. He did occasionally acknowledge the presence of small farmers, but he portrayed them as a kind of endangered species who, by subsiding slowly into destitution, were illustrating the superiority of the slave plantation as a means of agricultural production. But as Frank Owsley argued in 1949, "the core of the social structure [of the old South] was a massive body of plain folk who were neither rich nor very poor." Nor did these plain folk—"that great mass of several millions who were not part of the plantation economy"—suffer economically. In their desire and ability to rise in station, they participated as fully in the American ethic of success as Ben Franklin, Jay Gatsby, or any Alger prototype in a northern city. Having surveyed the tax records of seven southern states between 1850 and 1860 (the major phase of Fitzhugh's career as an interpreter of the South), Owsley found that "hardly a single family failed to ascend the economic ladder."[27] It was, in fact,

---

26. Bruce, *Violence and Culture in the Antebellum South,* 4; Greenberg, *Masters and Statesmen,* 144–46.

27. Owsley, *Plain Folk,* 7–8; McWhiney, Introduction, *ibid.,* viii. Owsley's method of analysis and several of his conclusions were forcefully challenged by Fabian Linden

these prospering yeomen who increasingly made up the ranks of the planter class—the putative aristocracy in which Fitzhugh placed his hopes; many (and eventually most) of the slaveholding planters of the Old South had risen from the ranks of the "plain folk."

Who were these folk? Fitzhugh barely concedes their existence, but we can get a sense of the actual range of southern society by considering the work of one of his contemporaries, the Alabama writer Daniel Hundley. In his *Social Relations in Our Southern States* (1860), Hundley offered a fascinating anatomy of southern social types, including not only "The Southern Gentleman" but also "The Cotton Snob," a parvenu clumsily attempting the manner of the aristocracy; not only the admirable "Southern Yeoman" but also his unprepossessing counterparts "The Southern Bully" and "Poor White Trash." Hundley anticipated Owsley by declaring that "as in all civilized countries, the middle classes of the South constitute the greater proportion of her citizens, and are likewise the most useful members of her society." His portrait of these classes shows us a people who—though of poor education and modest means—were nonetheless ambitious, jealous of their rights, and inclined to defer to nobody. "For mark you," he says, "[the middle-class southerner] is a man of stoutest independence, always carries a bold and open front; asks no favors of either friend or foe, and would no sooner doff his hat to the Autocrat of the Russias, than to his poor neighbor Tom Jones."[28]

As one might expect in a region populated by such folk, southern politics tended to be intensely democratic. In the South after 1830, says William J. Cooper, "democracy reigned," elective offices increasingly went to men from the lower and middle classes, and even such

---

in 1946, in an article often cited as a refutation of the "plain folk" argument. But though Linden exposes many inadequacies in Owsley's statistical methods, he acknowledges the continuing validity of Owsley's basic assertion that "there was a substantial number of small and medium sized property owners in the slave South" and that "the old planter–poor white stereotype of southern society" is therefore "an outmoded fiction." See Linden, "Economic Democracy in the Slave South," *Journal of Negro History*, XXXI (1946), 140–89.

28. Daniel R. Hundley, *Social Relations in Our Southern States*, ed. William J. Cooper, Jr. (Baton Rouge, 1979), 78, 84.

aristocrats as remained in power were forced to recognize "the growing power of an increasingly broad based and active voting public." By the mid-1830s all but two southern states had dropped the property-holding requirement for suffrage. Any adult white male was entitled to vote, and most were inclined to do so: in both the 1840 and the 1844 presidential elections voter turnout in the South was 75 percent. Hundley—who was in a position to know, having attended Harvard and lived in Chicago—believed that even the poorest southerners were more politically alert than most northerners, thanks to the educational value of "public barbecues, court-house day gatherings, and other holiday occasions, which are more numerous in the South than in the North." To appeal to these democrats, Cooper concludes, "politicians and both political parties constantly sang hymns glorifying the sovereignty of the people."[29]

As for the South's alleged freedom from marketplace values, one simply has to recall on what the region's economic well-being was based. If cotton was king, as James Henry Hammond said, it was because the world economic market exerted a powerful demand for that crop, as it did for sugar and rice and tobacco, the other principal southern exports. Southerners invariably involved themselves in the capitalist logic of the marketplace whenever they sold those crops—indeed, whenever they employed such marvels of technology as the cotton gin to produce them. It is true that Fitzhugh's Virginia, growing little cotton and lagging behind in all agricultural production, was somewhat less implicated in this world market than was the Deep South. But it was precisely because of this circumstance that Virginia was able to enter enthusiastically into another market: it began the massive exportation of slaves, of whom there were too many on the economically sluggish seaboard and too few in the booming Southwest. Of course, many southerners did approach Fitzhugh's ideal of freedom from the marketplace, but they were precisely the ones whose very existence he tried to deny: the small farmers, most of whom never

29. Cooper, *Liberty and Slavery*, 184–85; Hundley, *Social Relations*, 201. The exceptions were Louisiana, which granted white male suffrage in 1845, and Fitzhugh's own Virginia, which did so in 1851.

managed much more than a comfortable subsistence. But to insist on the plantation's freedom from the marketplace, at the very moment of Hammond's coronation of King Cotton and from the heart of perhaps the greatest slave market in the world, required of Fitzhugh a special heedlessness to the world around him.

All of this is to say that if chaos and flux were the great social evils Fitzhugh meant to attack, he hardly needed to venture all the way to New England to find them. Why did he do so, while maintaining that at home there prevailed a peaceful, aristocratic, and antimaterialist order? His sincere desire to defend slavery does not fully account for it; few other proslavery writers found it necessary to claim such utopian virtues for their region. Neither, I shall argue, does ignorance account for it. Even if Fitzhugh managed, by some yogi-like feat of concentration, to ignore the social circumstances I have just described, he could hardly have ignored the circumstances of his own life and that of his family. For the Fitzhughs of Virginia were among the principal victims of this dynamic, Jacksonian South.

George Fitzhugh's first American ancestor, William Fitzhugh, had emigrated from Bedfordshire to Virginia in 1671, bringing with him title to some ninety-six thousand acres in the Northern Neck. This patriarch—whom his descendant later described as "a fair classical scholar, a learned, able, and industrious lawyer, a high tory, a high churchman"—established large plantations in northern Virginia for each of his five sons, who began establishing something of a Fitzhugh dynasty in that region. The Fitzhughs were, a later historian noted, "universally esteemed for their talent, probity, and high morality." But by the time of George's birth, on November 4, 1806, the family had fallen considerably in the world. This decline was owing in part to the generally depressed economy of seaboard Virginia in these years. Between 1817 and 1829 land values in the region fell by more than half, while exports declined by two-thirds. In the following decade, thanks to this economic malaise, eastern Virginia lost some twenty-six thousand inhabitants, most of them moving west in search of prosperity. Fitzhugh himself was raised on a large but money-losing plantation in King George County; when his father died in 1825, the land had to be sold at a cash auction to satisfy the dead man's many creditors.

Unlike his ancestor, Fitzhugh received no classical education; he was educated at a "field school" and then trained for a career at law. Eventually, by marrying well, he was able to acquire a plantation of sorts—"a rickety old mansion," a neighbor called it, "situated on the fag-end of a once noble estate"—but his livelihood depended on his law practice.[30] All of this is to say that he managed, at best, only a very rough approximation of the old southern ideal of the republican farmer, rooted securely on his land.

Likewise, the political power which by tradition belonged to a Virginian of his background eluded George Fitzhugh all his life. The politics of the state had changed; the days when a wealthy planter like John Taylor could be swept into office by virtual acclamation, without troubling to campaign, were over. In 1851 Virginia finally abandoned its ancient restriction of the franchise to property owners, concluding a tropism toward wider democracy that had begun at the 1829 Constitutional Convention. The new dispensation, offering the vote to all white men, permitted the rise of a species of democratic populism in the Old Dominion. "Almost any ruffian," said Hundley, "who would ply the rabble strong enough with flattery, could be elected to the Virginia Assembly over the heads of the most able and refined of the First Families." The successful politician was now expected to flatter and cajole the voters, to throw barbecues and press the flesh, activities for which the dreamy, reserved Fitzhugh had little taste and less talent. When he finally tried his hand at a political career, he found himself just barely able to translate a lifetime's loyalty to the Democratic party into a modest patronage job in the Buchanan administration. At the time he wrote his first proslavery tract, Fitzhugh was practicing law halfheartedly—he confessed to a "horror at the approach of clients . . . as natural and universal as the dread of snakes"—and spending most of his time reading magazines and daydreaming.[31]

To contemplate Fitzhugh's situation in 1849—a forty-three-year-old unsuccessful lawyer, scion of a distinguished but nearly defunct Virginia family, an intelligent man aspiring in vain to a place of importance in

30. Wish, *George Fitzhugh*, 6, 13.
31. Hundley, *Social Relations*, 83; Wish, *George Fitzhugh*, 19.

his country—is to begin understanding the appeal his particular version of southern identity must have had for him. Small wonder he
preferred to wish away so many disagreeable facts about his region, to
believe that, contrary to appearances, the South was not peopled by
stubbornly egalitarian democrats, was not evangelically Protestant,
alive with the rhythms of camp meetings, did not display the disdain
for aristocrats and intellectuals which one would expect of a democratic, agrarian culture. How much more pleasant to believe in a feudal
South, built on elaborate patterns of economic, social, and political
hierarchy, populated chiefly by happy slaves and virtuous masters, with
a necessary handful of philosophers like himself, engaged in isolating
the essential truths embodied by the southern regime and receiving
honor, gratitude, and power for doing so. Did Fitzhugh believe what
he said of his region? It is impossible to say; but at best, one suspects,
his belief in this regional image must have been a rather fragile thing,
kept carefully isolated from his daily experience of the Jacksonian
South. In his public behavior, however, Fitzhugh never acknowledged
any doubts, never appeared to let the more unpleasant facts about his
region—including its notable indifference to himself and his work—
shake his conviction.

In his background, Fitzhugh was typical of southern proslavery intellectuals. David Donald, in a well-known essay, has argued that the
typical apologist for slavery was aristocratic by background, intellectual
by inclination, and largely excluded from power in a region given over
to Jacksonian democracy. The intellectual defense of slavery was as
much as anything an effort to persuade the region of the value of its
dispossessed elite; they were the ones who could answer Yankee critics
in kind and defend the *Patria* against its enemies. Indeed, as Donald
has shown in a related essay, the situation of these southern aristocrats
had its nearest American parallel precisely in that of the people they
promised to refute, the abolitionists of the North. The New England
aristocracy of the age, Donald argues—"descended from old and socially dominant Northeastern families, reared in a faith of aggressive
piety and moral endeavor, educated for conservative leadership"—was
"an elite without a function, a displaced class" in a society increasingly
dominated by the bustle of business. Many of these New Englanders

expressed their distaste for the age and their desire for a return to a more virtuous past by becoming abolitionists, a persuasion that offered vent to both their moral acuteness and their hatred of the age of manufacture, which they associated not only with the mills of Lowell but also with the southern cotton fields that supplied them. "Basically," Donald concludes, "abolitionism should be considered the anguished protest of an aggrieved class against a world they never made."[32]

The parallel implied by Donald's two essays offers one of the best ways to begin understanding George Fitzhugh—understanding him, that is, as a nineteenth-century American writer rather than an inexplicable throwback to the age of William the Conqueror. It permits us, for example, to consider him in relation to that American generation whose history Ralph Waldo Emerson recounted in his late essay "Historic Notes of Life and Letters in New England"; indeed, Emerson's essay inadvertently offers one of the best glosses on Fitzhugh's career. "The ancient manners were giving way," said Emerson of the age. "The stockholder has stepped into the place of the warlike baron. The nobles shall not any longer, as feudal lords, have power of life and death over the churls, but now, in another shape, as capitalists, shall in all love and peace eat them up as before"—cannibals all, as Fitzhugh said. In response to these developments, the young New Englander was "driven to find all his resources, hopes, rewards, society and deity within himself"; thus "the young men were born with knives in their brain, a tendency to introversion, self-dissection, anatomizing of motives."[33]

Such was the fate of New England's aristocrats—some of them, at least—in a world of chaos, flux, and materialism. It was, *mutatis mutandis,* also the world in which George Fitzhugh lived; and his responses to it were not altogether different from those of his contemporaries. Failing in most of his attempts to win his way in the world—as a planter, a politician, or a lawyer—Fitzhugh too turned inward; he tried

---

32. David Donald, "The Proslavery Argument Reconsidered," *Journal of Southern History,* XXXVII (1971), 4–18; Donald, "Toward a Reconsideration of Abolitionists," in *Lincoln Reconsidered* (New York, 1961).

33. Ralph Waldo Emerson, "Historic Notes on Life and Letters in New England," in *Lectures and Biographical Sketches,* 325, 328, 329.

to establish himself as a man of letters, hoping that culture was the place where the line would hold and order would be preserved. Echoing the tone of Emerson's "Historic Notes," Fitzhugh's acquaintance Moncure D. Conway (a friend of Emerson's, incidentally) recalled that these years were "a time when a 'Young Virginia' was rising up to promulgate the philosophical, sociological, and ethical excellence of slavery." It was, he said, "the most scholarly and philosophical young men who discarded old Virginia principles and advocated slavery *per se*."[34]

The New England aristocrats who became Transcendentalists were crucially affected by their encounter with new European thinkers: with Immanuel Kant, Emanuel Swedenborg, Samuel Taylor Coleridge, and, perhaps most important, Carlyle. The same was true for Fitzhugh. Carlyle was the great influence on his work: many of his pithiest phrases and both the title and subtitle of his second book were borrowed from the Scots eccentric. Behind Fitzhugh's discovery of most men's "inalienable right to be slaves," for instance, was Carlyle's declaration of "the everlasting privilege of the foolish to be governed by the wise." Behind his innumerable attacks on liberalism as the cause of social disintegration, one discovers Carlyle's demolition of the notion

> that the grand panacea for social woes is what we call "enfranchisement," "emancipation"; or, translated into practical language, the cutting asunder of human relations, wherever they are found to be grievous, as is like to be pretty universally the case at the rate we have been going for some generations past. Let us all be "free" of one another; we shall then be happy. Free, without bond or connection except that of cash payment; fair day's wages for the fair day's work; bargained for by voluntary contract, and law of supply-and-demand: this is thought to be the true solution of all difficulties and injustices that have occurred between man and man.

And again:

> Cut every human relation which has anywhere grown uneasy sheer asunder; reduce whatsoever was compulsory to voluntary, whatsoever was permanent among us to the condition of nomadic:—in other words,

34. Wish, *George Fitzhugh*, 44.

loosen by assiduous wedges in every joint, the whole fabric of social existence, stone from stone; till at last, all now being loose enough, it can, as we already see in most countries, be overset by sudden outburst of revolutionary rage; and lying as mere mountains of anarchic rubbish, solicit you sing Fraternity etc. over it, and to rejoice in the new remarkable era of human progress we have arrived at.[35]

Equally important to Fitzhugh's development (and here his experience departs from that of the New Englanders) was his discovery of the works of the European reactionaries who had attempted, in the wake of the French Revolution, to reconstitute social order by isolating its essential components and in the process invented the new discipline of sociology. In 1854 Fitzhugh became the first American writer to employ the neologism "sociology."[36] The early sociologists were attempting, as Robert Nisbet argues, to manage a paradox: to attempt, by intensely conscious effort, to restore a traditional order that was by its nature unconscious. "The sign of health is unconsciousness," said Carlyle; and Karl Mannheim observed that in conservative thought "the simple habit of living more or less unconsciously, as though the old ways of life were still appropriate, gradually gives way to a deliberate effort to maintain them under new conditions, and they are raised to the level of conscious reflection, of deliberate 'recollection.'"[37] The drama in many of the early works of European sociology, as in the writing of their American disciple George Fitzhugh, is that of Mannheim's self-conscious conservatism attempting to become—through the alchemy offered by the new science of society—Carlyle's "unconsciousness." These sociologists thought of the traditional order of Europe as a kind of inheritance, but an inheritance that one had to work at inheriting.

So it was for Fitzhugh. We find in his work a series of antitheses,

---

35. Carlyle, "The Present Time," 23–25.

36. Fitzhugh was actually tied for this honor by another proslavery writer, Henry Hughes, Mississippi-born author of *Treatise on Sociology* (1854).

37. Robert Nisbet, *The Sociological Tradition* (New York, 1966); Carlyle, "Characteristics," in *Critical and Miscellaneous Essays*, Vol. III (New York, 1900), 4; Karl Mannheim, "The Meaning of Conservatism," in *Essays on Sociology and Social Psychology* (London, 1953), 115.

operating in a curious but fruitful tension: antiquity and modernity, conservatism and progressivism, a profound regard for the *status quo* and an essentially imperialistic desire to remake it according to a pre-conceived ideal. This cast of Fitzhugh's mind may be perceived, I think, even in the form of his arguments. Anyone who has read him has noted his perfect willingness to contradict himself whenever the rhetorical situation demands it: at one moment he tells us that the South languishes in poverty because it farms and that the North prospers because it manufactures; a moment later he is claiming unrivaled prosperity for the slaveholding South and describing, with unconcealed glee, the grim privation endured by freedom-loving Yankees. Fitzhugh was a careless writer, which no doubt helps to account for these internal contradictions. But it does not wholly explain them, any more than it explains the same rhetorical habit in Whitman or Emerson. In all three cases these contradictions express (and are meant to express) the superiority of conception to mere circumstance: of mind, we might say, to history. For Fitzhugh as for his northern contemporaries, there were exalted moments when the facts of experience seemed infinitely malleable, when the blank page before him conferred not just absolute freedom but absolute power. Fitzhugh's willingness to contradict himself, like his willingness to ignore so much of the social reality of his region, was the assertion of what Quentin Anderson has called an "imperial self" against a recalcitrant outside world.

My impression is that we can most profitably think of Fitzhugh not as a political thinker—in that capacity he was derivative, confused, and largely without influence—but as an imaginative writer. Rather than compare him to, say, John Calhoun, who was surely a more systematic and original political philosopher, we ought to think of him in relation to thinkers like Whitman and Lincoln, minds not just powerful but aggressive, attempting to save their country by radically re-imagining it. Fitzhugh—floating free of all the troublesome circumstances of the place he lived and flourishing in a utopian ideal called "the South"—is engaged in the same project that Lincoln outlined in his famous Springfield Lyceum speech and carried out in his announcement at Gettysburg of a "new birth of freedom": a radical refounding of the country. Fitzhugh is asking the South more or less what

Whitman asked of the Union in "Long, Too Long America": "Who, except myself, has yet conceived what your children enmasse really are?" All three thinkers are asserting—with, perhaps, a measure of heroism, given the troubles all had faced—the supremacy of mind.

Whitman and Lincoln are odd company, perhaps, for a man who grew up within a stone's throw of John Taylor's Hazelwood and counted himself an admirer of the old agrarian. Taylor, after all, was the man who insisted so doggedly on the importance of details and who could barely bring himself to utter an abstract idea. And yet it is perhaps not so odd, for as Taylor himself knew, the pastoral republican persuasion was in constant danger of deteriorating into a merely utopian vision. Much of his work was meant to pull against this tendency. Republicanism was founded, after all, on an essential fear of history and a belief that it might somehow be evaded by a retreat into the past, or the West, or finally the mind. This last refuge was where John Randolph ended his career and where Beverley Tucker—for all his efforts to gain a hearing in the wider world—spent nearly all of his. Fitzhugh was their legitimate heir, though none of the parties, including Fitzhugh, might have wished to own the connection. Though he never ceased proclaiming his originality (a claim that was itself a version of the republican habit of denying history), Fitzhugh throughout his career followed the path laid down by his republican predecessors.

When the Civil war finally came, Fitzhugh, for all his regional chauvinism, regretted it; oddly, he was never much of a southern nationalist. But he was, as always, able to adjust to circumstances, supporting the southern cause dutifully and supplying, in a series of essays in *De Bow's Review*, a rationale for the war effort. And when, four years later, the Confederacy came to an end, Fitzhugh again landed on his feet. In a way his resilience is remarkable. His fellow southern partisan and proslavery theorist Edmund Ruffin, when he saw that defeat was inevitable, wrapped himself in a Confederate flag, penned a letter declaring his undying hatred of "the perfidious, malignant, & vile Yankee race," and blew his brains out. Fitzhugh went out and secured an administrative job in—incredible as it seems—the Freedmen's Bureau. He would, of course, have denied that any self-contradiction was involved in this step: his defense of slavery, so he had always maintained, was founded on a tender concern for the welfare of slaves; now that they were free, he would protect them as well as he could from the terrible consequences of freedom. At the same time, he went on writing on the subject of race and hierarchy, arguing now that only some new form of slavery, within the guidelines of the Thirteenth Amendment, could secure the happiness of the freedmen; left alone to compete in a free market, they would soon be destroyed.

It seems appropriate that Fitzhugh, who had spent his life as a prophet of the southern future, ended his days in the Southwest—the landscape that for him and others had symbolized that future. After the death of his wife in 1877, he moved to Frankfort, Kentucky, to live with a son; two years later he moved still further west, to Huntsville, Texas, where his daughter and son-in-law lived. He reportedly retained in his last years, though ill and eventually blind, the cheerfulness and habitual optimism that had marked his entire career. Remarkably unembittered by a lifetime of disappointment, he impressed observers as "a man of even temper and perfect self control, full of quiet kindness and as absent minded as any professor was ever supposed to be."[38] He died in Huntsville in 1881 at age seventy-four.

38. Wish, *George Fitzhugh*, 340.

5

Joseph Glover Baldwin and the Language of Virtue

Nearly all the antebellum theorists of southern identity shared Fitzhugh's interest in the western frontier. John Taylor regarded it and the restless progressivism underlying the impulse of western expansion as threats to republican order; like-minded John Randolph boasted that he had never voted to admit a new state to the Union. Other republicans, believing that republican virtue depended on land and seeing the West as a vast source of arable acres, had considered western expansion as the main hope for the perpetuation of republicanism in America. Of course, this interest in the West as the landscape of the future was not exclusively southern; during the period when much of America's energy was directed to territorial expansion, the pace of westward movement seemed to many Americans a clear indicator of national progress. And as the sectional conflict began to take shape during the Missouri dispute, northerners as well as southerners began to take a new interest in the West; the struggle over the status of slavery in the western territories was for forty years the most obvious locus of sectional tension. Americans of both regions instinctively understood that the fate of slavery in the West somehow predicted its fortunes in the country at large. But it is probably true that the South regarded the frontier with especially urgent interest: if the West was for many Americans a symbol of the future, then the South—apparently declining in power and moral standing, its future in considerable doubt— had particular reason to survey the terrain carefully. It is no wonder that Beverley Tucker and George Fitzhugh, those prophets of southern destiny, remained all their lives fascinated by the southern frontier and its prospects and no wonder that most of their kindred southern millennialists made western expansion a major component of the glorious southern destiny they predicted.

But the southern writers best known for their portrayals of the West were not grimly earnest southern nationalists but humorists, and they usually published their accounts not in fire-eating journals like *Russell's* or *De Bow's* but in lowly sporting magazines with no pretension to high purpose. Beginning, it is conventional to say, with Augustus Baldwin Longstreet's *Georgia Scenes* (1835), the humorists of the Old Southwest created a remarkable body of writing describing the conditions of life on the southern frontier. They included a college professor from Georgia, a physician from Louisiana, a newspaperman from East Tennessee, and—the subject of this chapter—a Virginia-born lawyer and Whig politician, unwillingly transplanted to the Alabama-Mississippi frontier.

Kenneth Lynn has taught us that these writers were usually professional men and gentlemen; in politics they tended to be Whigs, which is to say rationalists and moderates, distressed by the excesses of Jacksonian democracy and secessionist fire-eating. We are now accustomed to read their works as being informed by a tension between the wildness of rustic characters like Ransy Sniffle, Simon Suggs, or Sut Lovingood and the civilized norms represented by the voice of the narrator, usually an eastern gentleman alternately shocked and amused by the frontier.[1] This tension is, of course, essentially political, and many of the humorists were professionally and avocationally interested in politics. But though this is so, and though most of the humorists were intensely southern in their loyalties, it is rare to find in their works much comment about the sectional crisis—a reflection, perhaps, of their Whiggish moderation or simply of their need to publish in northern journals. The closest most of them come to sectional politics is telling, with palpable relish, a version of one of the more common southwestern "grinning" stories, that of the Yankee schoolmaster terrorized by southern ruffians. On the face of it, they may seem to have little relevance for a study of the literature of southern destiny.

But there is a connection, I believe. To begin with, the intrinsic

1. Kenneth S. Lynn, *Mark Twain and Southwestern Humor* (Boston, 1959).

significance of their subject matter meant that the humorists inevitably touched on the topic of southern destiny, whether they meant to or not, whenever they ventured an observation about life on the southern frontier. But many of them, I think, were aware that their position on the frontier gave them a unique leverage in the intrasectional debate. Lewis Simpson, introducing the second edition of his classic study *The Dispossessed Garden*, makes a suggestive argument along these lines. He maintains that the generally bleak portrait of the southern pastoral realm created by the humorists was "an antipastoral allegory of American history," carrying "the force of a treasonous political statement." The humorists subvert, he adds, "an American politics of pastoral grounded in the expectation that America is a pastoral intervention in the long unhappy history of man in the metropolis of Europe."[2] My own impression of this literature is a bit different from Simpson's. I believe that the humorists often undermine pastoral conventions but seldom betray the pastoral republican vision; as I shall explain shortly, I think that antipastoral writing often turns out to be a version of the old pastoral impulse. But Simpson is exactly right that the work of the humorists amounts to a radical critique of the American (and specifically southern) pastoral myth in both its Edenic and its millennial versions. Having glimpsed firsthand the landscape of southern destiny, they issued reports on the experience which rather rudely deflated the more exuberant anticipations of the future and, by implication, endorsed instead the more modest hopes of the old Virginia republicans. This is particularly true of one of the best of these humorists and one of the most sophisticated in his application of pastoral and republican principles to the question of southern destiny: the author of *The Flush Times of Alabama and Mississippi*, Joseph Glover Baldwin.

Baldwin was a Virginian, born in 1815 in the Shenandoah Valley. Though the descendant of Connecticut Yankees who had migrated south after the American Revolution, Jo Baldwin imbibed in youth, and retained all his life, an extraordinary pride in his Virginia birth and an unquestioning faith in Virginia political principles. After at-

2. Lewis P. Simpson, *The Dispossessed Garden: Pastoral and History in Southern Literature* (2nd ed.; Baton Rouge, 1983), xii.

tending Staunton Academy, where he was the rather unwilling recipient of a decent classical education, he undertook legal studies, meanwhile supporting himself by coediting a Lexington newspaper with his brother Cornelius. When Jo's strong "state-rights" principles brought him into conflict with his fellow editor, the young journalist moved on to a position as editor and chief correspondent of a neighboring town's paper, the Buchanan *Advocate and Commercial Gazette*. In an early issue of this four-page weekly—which was devoted mainly to racetrack news, jokes, recipes, and local gossip—the twenty-one-year-old Baldwin grandly announced that his paper was beholden to no "party" and that "the senior editor intends . . . to speak with the boldness of a free man."[3] John Randolph would have approved both the sentiment and the dramatic flourish.

His legal studies concluded, Baldwin retired from journalism and attempted to establish himself in his chosen profession but found his efforts in vain. Economic disaster was fairly common in Virginia in these days; opportunities for an ambitious young man—as Beverley Tucker had discovered a few years earlier—were limited, owing to what Baldwin called a "surplus of talent" in the Old Dominion. Thus at the age of twenty-one, Baldwin found himself (again like Tucker) compelled to move to the southern frontier, "urged by hunger and the request of friends," he explained.[4] Instead of Missouri, Baldwin elected the cotton-growing Deep South; he arrived at DeKalb, Mississippi, near the Alabama line, in April, 1836.

The young Virginian was surprised to find himself admitted to the Mississippi bar by a circuit court judge who asked him "not a single legal question" (51). The ease of admission to the state bar and the peculiar social circumstances of a new country—speculation run wild, business conducted mainly on credit, murder and mayhem common-

---

3. There is, unfortunately, no published biography of Baldwin. The best source of information on his life and the one I have principally drawn upon is Samuel Boyd Stewart, "Joseph Glover Baldwin" (Ph.D. dissertation, Vanderbilt University, 1941), quotation on 49.

4. Joseph Glover Baldwin, *The Flush Times of Alabama and Mississippi: A Series of Sketches by Joseph G. Baldwin*. Introduction by James Justus. (1853; rpr. Baton Rouge, 1987), 47. Hereafter cited in the text by page number.

place—made the southern frontier an attractive place for a young bar-rister: "a California of Law," Baldwin called it, "a legal Utopia, peopled by a race of eager litigants, only waiting for the lawyers to come on and divide out to them the shells of a bountiful system of squabbling" (47–48). Soon Baldwin, who unlike many southwestern lawyers could have passed a legal examination had one been required, established himself as a leader of the bar in DeKalb and later in Sumter County, Alabama, just across the state line. In 1843, with his legal practice secure, Baldwin developed an interest in politics, winning a seat in the Alabama House of Representatives. By 1848 he had become a promi-nent Alabama Whig, serving as a delegate at the party's national con-vention, campaigning enthusiastically for Zachary Taylor, and finally running for the U.S. Congress. He narrowly lost that race and left politics, not to hold office again for another ten years; instead, like Tucker and Fitzhugh after their political disappointments, he turned to literature.

In 1851 he began submitting humorous sketches, recollections of his early days as a frontier lawyer, to the *Southern Literary Messenger*—a much more prestigious venue than the sporting magazines in which frontier humor usually appeared, indicating something of Baldwin's fundamentally serious purpose in writing. The magazine published nineteen of Baldwin's sketches in three years, after which the editor, John R. Thompson, suggested that they be collected between hard covers. Together the two found a New York publisher, D. Appleton & Co., and *The Flush Times of Alabama and Mississippi* was published in December, 1853. It was an immediate success, which led Thompson to suggest, with Appleton's strong encouragement, that Baldwin put together another collection, this one of the serious essays on American political history which he had lately begun publishing in the *Messenger*. By the summer of 1854 he had prepared the volume that was published the following year as *Party Leaders*; it contained biographical sketches of Jefferson, Hamilton, Randolph, Jackson, and Clay, as well as a gen-eral account of American politics from the founding to the present day.

The brief flurry of writing and publishing from 1851 to 1854 was essentially the whole of Baldwin's literary career; law and politics again became his chief interests, and though near the end of his life he began work on another series of humorous sketches, he never completed another book. What are we to make of that career? A genial, rambling memoir of youth and a deadly serious history of American politics: on the face of it a rather uneven performance, from which it is difficult to make any inference about a larger purpose in his writing. And yet the two books are related; together, I think, they constitute Baldwin's effort—the effort of an old-fashioned Virginia republican, born a generation too late—to understand the condition of his country and region in the years immediately before the Civil War.

We ought to begin by considering the intellectual equipment Baldwin brought to this inquiry. As a boy, we are told, he displayed a strong taste for literature, which (as commonly happened to promising young men in the nineteenth century) was eventually turned toward the study of law. In the early years of the republic, as Robert Ferguson has shown, law was unequaled as a path to wealth and prominence: all of America was once "a California of law." "Men of talents in this country," said Virginia lawyer William Wirt in 1803, "have been generally bred to the profession of the law, and indeed throughout the United States, I have met with few persons of exalted intellect, whose powers have been directed to any other pursuit. The bar in America is the road to honour."[5] A legal education in the early nineteenth century, particularly in Virginia, meant an education in republican principles. Sir William Blackstone's four-volume *Commentaries on the Laws of England* was by far the most important text in American legal education, and a student who took his Blackstone to heart learned above all a reverence for common law—which is to say a respect for history and tradition, for what Patrick Henry called "the lamp of experience," as the source of liberty and social wisdom.[6] It is likely that Baldwin, like many Virginia law students, used the critical edition of the *Commentaries* edited by St. George Tucker and thus got his Blackstone with a decidedly southern republican twist: Tucker's textual apparatus included his own

5. Quoted in Ferguson, *Law and Letters*, 12.
6. On the importance of history to the republican persuasion, see Colbourn, *Lamp of Experience*.

thoughts on the Virginia Constitution, a brief in behalf of states' rights, and even his plan for the elimination of slavery. The architects of Virginia pastoral republicanism were, of course, nearly all lawyers, and Virginia lawyers took it as their particular calling to defend that body of thought in the national arena. In *The Flush Times* Baldwin refers with affectionate irony to the Virginia lawyer's habit of resolving all philosophical issues by adverting to "those Eleusinian mysteries, the [Virginia and Kentucky] Resolutions of 1798–99" (24). A Virginia-trained lawyer, that is, was prepared as a defender of pastoral republican principles. Certainly this was true of Baldwin himself. His biographer, Samuel Boyd Stewart, points out that the sacred phrase "state-rights" is always capitalized in Baldwin's writing and that "Jo was a Whig and an ardent state-rights man." "He changed political parties once," Stewart concludes, "but he never shifted his principles." [7]

More broadly, as Ferguson shows, such a lawyer had been immersed in a legal epistemology founded on "the bond between literature, general knowledge, and law." [8] American lawyers were expected to be broadly learned, not just narrowly trained. The result, as Ferguson shows, was that these lawyers displayed as a professional trait a remarkably high degree of intellectual and moral assurance. They had been taught to believe in the power of law—and in their own power—to comprehend chaos and impose order upon it. Thus lawyers considered themselves to have a particularly important role to play in a new country like America. Baldwin, fully sharing this belief, observes in *The Flush Times* that "the first thing our fathers did was to get a country; then to fix on it the character of government it was to have; then to make laws to carry it on and achieve its objects. The men, as a class, who did all this, were lawyers." (224).

Ferguson also points out that this ideal of the lawyer as omnicompetent generalist was beginning to die out by the 1830s, when Baldwin was taking up legal studies. Law schools had proliferated, and the law was being defined more narrowly as a profession. But Baldwin himself was largely untouched by these reforms; living in the rustic Shen-

---

7. Stewart, "Joseph Glover Baldwin," 33, 53.
8. Ferguson, *Law and Letters*, 28.

andoah Valley, he received a fairly archaic legal education—one by apprenticeship, at the knee of an older lawyer, his uncle Briscoe G. Baldwin. He learned his law, that is, in the way that John Taylor had learned his and in a way that fewer and fewer young men were doing by the 1830s. When he left Virginia, carrying his Blackstone and a few dollars in his saddlebags, Baldwin brought with him a set of assumptions about law and politics which would in many quarters have been considered outmoded. We might think of him as an anachronism, a belated eighteenth-century Virginian, on his way to meet the frontier.

As it happened, his archaic professional training served him well there. For on the frontier (to cite Ferguson's findings one more time), the old-fashioned legal generalist was better prepared than the modern professional to survive and prosper. The law was still taking shape in such regions, local precedent was almost nonexistent (making it necessary for lawyers and judges to rely on general legal knowledge), and specialization was unheard-of: a young barrister had better be prepared for whatever sort of case came his way. And so Baldwin prospered; the legal profession served him as it was supposed to, propelling an able young man to wealth and position.

It is important to remember Baldwin's experience in the law when considering him in relation to the other Virginia lawyers I have discussed in previous chapters. For in experience as well as in schooling, Baldwin resembled an eighteenth-century man like John Taylor more than he did contemporaries like Tucker and Fitzhugh. For Baldwin, as for Taylor, the law had proven a secure path to honor and wealth; everything in both men's experiences tended to bolster their confidence in the republican lawyer's worldview. Tucker and Fitzhugh, in contrast, though they had also been immersed in that worldview at an early age, were taught very different lessons by adult experience. Both of them found the Virginia bar a diminished thing, crowded with ill-trained pretenders who, maddeningly, seemed to succeed in spite of their unfitness. Fitzhugh never achieved much success in law or politics, and Tucker did so only after years of disappointment and then only by removing from Virginia to the Missouri frontier. It seems that these experiences somewhat undermined both men's faith in law and republicanism as touchstones of civil life. It is clear in any case that they both—though deeply marked by their republican educations—eventually began to search elsewhere for sources of order.

To understand Tucker's and Fitzhugh's abandonment of the legal-republican epistemology, it is useful to recall Perry Miller's argument that in America between the Revolution and the Civil War law as a principle of social order competed for influence with evangelical religion.[9] The one body of thought offered the promise of gradual progress toward a better social order, a progress founded on reason and the provisional truths of precedent and statute; the other held forth the possibility of immediate contact with final truths and sought a radical transformation of society in the light of Christian revelation. We might think of Tucker and Fitzhugh as lawyers who (like Charles Grandison Finney, the lawyer who became the most famous nineteenth-century evangelist) abandoned legal modes of thought for the hope of immediate revelation and social transformation. Of course, neither Tucker nor Fitzhugh was primarily a religious thinker (though both were religious men). But their social teaching had in common with evangelical thought the promise of an approaching millennium, to be achieved by a radical social transformation; both men, by staking a preemptive claim on the future, sought an escape from the confusions of historical process by predicting a golden age in which that process would simply cease: the end of history, ushered in by a triumphant South.[10]

Such a promise was, as we have seen, a significant departure from what John Taylor would have regarded as Virginia's republican tradition, with its emphasis on tradition, precedent, and the gradual, incremental accumulation of social wisdom and its hope not of escaping history but of taking one's stand within it. And it was considerably at variance with the social teaching of Joseph Glover Baldwin, a transplanted Virginian who remained steadfast in his commitment to that old tradition even as it—and the Union it had helped shape—began

9. Perry Miller, *The Life of the Mind in America: From the Revolution to the Civil War* (New York, 1965).

10. Nor were Tucker and Fitzhugh unique in this respect; on the prevalence of millennial thought in the Confederacy, see Drew Gilpin Faust, *The Creation of Confederate Nationalism: Ideology and Identity in the Civil War South* (Baton Rouge, 1988).

to crumble around him. I believe that Baldwin's two books, his humorous memoir and his serious political history, have in common their effort to understand the origins of this rival doctrine and to sustain, in behalf of the old republican view, an indictment against it.

Baldwin's theme in *The Flush Times* is essentially that of civilization besieged on the frontier, a theme which the author, from his vantage point in the courthouses of Alabama, was well situated to observe. For the most part he regards the frontier and the restless, westering impulse that created it pretty much as John Taylor had—as a threat to stable republican order. He differs from most republican analysts, including Taylor, chiefly in his understanding of how very much was at risk when the foundations of republican order were undermined. Thus beginning with comparatively small matters, the ones he constantly encountered in his law practice, he traces their implications outward until he is prepared to portray the basic nature of a society.

In its emphases, at least, Baldwin's account of the frontier differs from that of any other practitioner of southwestern humor. As James Justus has pointed out, the central figures of such fiction—"hunters, hog-merchants, ring-tailed roarers, gamblers, circuit riders"—are in *The Flush Times* consigned to the periphery, and its usual subjects— physical violence, depravity, the grotesque—are ignored altogether. Baldwin's main characters are all lawyers, and his principal concerns may be inferred from the terms that, as Justus suggests, recur most often in his vocabulary: "humbug, pretentiousness, fraud."[11]

As Baldwin experienced the frontier, its fundamental problem (and the one that made it a promising place for a young lawyer) was simply that its property relations were maddeningly complicated. It was an agricultural society, resting on the ideal of the freeholder—the individual "founded," as Pocock says, "in property." But during the "flush times," when speculation was the rule and nearly all transactions were managed on credit, debt was the common condition of life and nobody owned anything outright, least of all the land on which he lived. Indeed, land, the most secure form of property for Virginia republicans,

---

11. James Justus, Introduction to Baldwin, *Flush Times*, xviii–xix.

served in Alabama almost as a form of currency, traded back and forth, gambled with and speculated upon. Frontier folk, who had abandoned their old roots to come west, seemed unwilling to put down new ones after arriving there; a southwestern farmer had only a minimal invest-ment of either time or money in the land that supported him.

Any Virginia republican could foretell the consequences of this state of affairs. Without the stabilizing institution of secure landed property, the rest of the social order wobbled alarmingly. Thus, Baldwin reports, "Society was wholly unorganized: there was no restraining public opin-ion: the law was well-nigh powerless—and religion scarcely was heard of except as furnishing the oaths and *technics* of profanity" (84). Many citizens experienced this unformed state of society as a liberation from all the constraints imposed by prudence and social sanction—from civilization, we might say, and its discontents. Indeed, at length these pioneers came to declare their independence not just from civilization but from its source, the fallen condition of man; they regarded Alabama as a paradise lying somewhere between the state of nature and the Garden of Eden. Thus "the world saw a fair experiment of what it would have been, if the fiat had never been pronounced which decreed subsistence as the price of labor" (84).

The author sums up this attitude succinctly in the first sketch of his book, a portrait of the representative citizen of this realm: a man sin-gularly undaunted by the tyranny of facts, a champion liar, a shape-shifting master of metamorphoses appropriately named Ovid Bolus. "I cannot," says Baldwin, "trace the early history, much less the birth-place, pedigree, and juvenile associations of this worthy. Whence he or his forebears got his name or how, I don't know: but for the fact that it is to be inferred that he got it in infancy, I should have thought he borrowed it: he borrowed everything else he ever had, such things as he got under the credit system only excepted" (1–2). After ponder-ing for a time the question of Bolus' leading vice, Baldwin decides that it must be lying: "The truth," he explains, "was too small for him. Fact was too dry and common-place for the fervor of his genius. Besides, great as was his memory—for he even remembered the outlines of his chief lies—his invention was still larger" (3). The confidence man is, of course, a standard figure in frontier humor, but Bolus is more than another version of Simon Suggs, illustrating once again the value of "shiftiness" in a new country.[12] Bolus' dissembling is no mere trick of the confidence man's trade; it is the essence of his being. It reflects not merely a wish to deceive others but a disdain for facts as such, including those of his own birth and identity. He operates on a Gatsby-like faith that the past doesn't matter, that reality can be made over to suit the needs of the moment: "He had a great contempt for history and historians. . . . He had long torn down the partition wall between his imagination and his memory. He had long ceased to distinguish between the impressions made upon his mind by what came *from* it, and what came *to* it: all ideas were facts to him" (3–4). If the older southern republicans, trying to span the widening gap between "ideas and substances," were forced to assume ever more precarious poses, then Bolus (their legitimate heir, though they might not have wished to claim him) solves the problem by simply denying the gap ("all ideas were facts to him"). Like his Roman namesake, Ovid Bolus has taken as his great subject the transformation of reality by art ("How well he asserted the Spiritual over the Material!" [5]). In his devotion to mind as against history, he might even be an oblique figuring of the modern man of letters ("he belonged to a higher department of the fine arts, and to a higher class of professors of this sort of Belles Lettres" [3]) — as such a man might be perceived by a belated eighteenth-century whig.

Ovid Bolus, of course, was merely the most accomplished liar of the Alabama frontier; in a region whose principal social practice seems to have been fraud, many others were apparently not far behind him in their contempt for circumstance and history. Thus the ultimate failing of the society these people have created is that it is unprecedented. It not only lacks foundation in custom or tradition, declining to employ Patrick Henry's "lamp of experience"; it is founded explicitly upon the rejection of these things in favor of the promise of a limitless future. Nor is Bolus merely the representative citizen of Alabama; he embodies

---

12. Baldwin does offer his own tribute to Johnston Jones Hooper's most famous character in one of his lesser sketches. See "Simon Suggs, Jr., Esq.; A Legal Biography," in *Flush Times*, 114–41.

a new America, one Baldwin found perplexing and disturbing. After all, by the time Baldwin set about writing his memoir, the flush times he recounted were long gone. The southern frontier of the 1830s matters, for Baldwin, mainly as a symbol and pure expression of social pathologies that had become general in American life by the 1850s; Ovid Bolus is worth remembering because he embodies a perennial American heresy, one which, as Baldwin believed, had come to dominate American political life in the decade before the Civil War.

Even by the 1830s, when Baldwin arrived in the Southwest, this ideology was already gaining strength. This was after all the age of Andrew Jackson, the man who, as Baldwin believed, most perfectly embodied this dangerous political faith. The historical moment—the "post-heroic" moment described by George Forgie—was ripe for the assault of Jackson, Bolus, and their kind. By 1832 the last of the American founders had died, thus severing what Webster called "a great link, connecting us with former times." With these forceful embodiments of past virtue out of the way at last, the spiritual kin of Andrew Jackson and Ovid Bolus had begun remaking the republic according to their preferences—had begun, as Baldwin believed, tearing it apart. The country had forgotten its history, the lamp of experience, and had lost its way.

This development would have surprised none of Baldwin's Virginia republican ancestors; one can readily imagine how fiercely John Taylor would have denounced the political life of the 1850s and how confidently he would have settled the blame on northern capitalists and ideologues. Then Taylor would have held up the virtuous, pastoral South as the antidote to the maladies of the age: a familiar Tertium Quid gesture, to which Baldwin is surely tempted. But Baldwin is forced to recognize, as Taylor never quite was, that his region was in no sense immune to the virus he was attempting to understand and arrest; Ovid Bolus was not just an American but an identifiably southern type. His "contempt for history and historians," his faith in an infinitely malleable reality, is essentially the creed we have discovered at work in the thought of Tucker and Fitzhugh. Like those two prophets of southern destiny, Ovid Bolus represents a will to escape history and its consequences and to stake a claim on a future of infinite possibility.

And what of the figure whom Taylor would have offered as Ovid Bolus' antithesis, the virtuous citizen—ideally a Virginian—rooted on his acres and schooled in pastoral politics? Baldwin imaginatively tests this champion in *The Flush Times* and finds him wanting. Baldwin's frontier is densely populated with virtuous Virginians, well-versed in the Eleusinian mysteries of republicanism, and they prove no obstacle at all to the triumph of Ovid Bolus and his kin. Thus the sketch that most vividly illustrates the destructive power of frontier culture and the helplessness of old ideas to restrain it is a grimly hilarious exercise in irony called "How the Times Served the Virginians." The Virginians who made their way westward, as Baldwin describes them, should have been ideally suited to impose order on the frontier; certainly their obsessively antiquarian view of the world is the precise opposite of Alabama's history-denying ethos. Their pride in their origins and their willingness to contemplate those origins more or less constantly are their most notable traits of character. "I never knew a debate [among them] that did not start *ab urbe condita*," says Baldwin: "They not only went back to first principles, but to first times; nor did I ever hear a discussion in which old John Adams and Thomas Jefferson did not figure—as if an interminable dispute had been going on for so many generations between these disputatious personages; as if the quarrel had begun before time, but was not to end with it" (76). And yet for all their instinctive reverence for precedent, these Virginians prove singularly unable to contend with the world of the frontier: "But all the habits of his life, his taste, his associations, his education—everything—the trustingness of his disposition—his want of business qualifications—his sanguine temper—all that was Virginian in him, made him the prey, if not of imposture, at least of unfortunate speculations. . . . How *could* he believe that that stuttering, grammarless Georgian, who had never heard of the resolutions of '98, could beat him in a land trade?" (93). What Baldwin was saying about Virginia pastoral republicanism—and it must have been painful to say it, for a loyal Virginian who dedicated his book to "'The Old Folks at Home,' My Friends in the Valley of the Shenandoah"—was that it had become a moribund faith, more inclined to contemplate its glorious past than to grapple seriously with the present. The once formidable politics represented by "the resolutions of '98" had degenerated into a local sect; its sacred principles were now merely the private crotchets of a handful of nostalgics.

This bleak state of affairs—Ovid Bolus triumphant, Virginia pastoral republicans in headlong retreat—is essentially the "antipastoral allegory of American history" which Lewis Simpson detects in the tradition of southwestern humor. But in Baldwin's case the matter is somewhat more complicated. For the author did not reject the essential themes of the old pastoral republican creed; his ideal of citizenship, a subject to which he gave considerable thought, emphasized precisely the virtues taught by John Taylor and his followers: independence, public-spiritedness, and honor. But Baldwin saw—even as Randolph, Tucker, and Fitzhugh had seen—that somehow Virginia, and the southern pastoral realm generally, had ceased to sustain these virtues. Southerners were now dividing themselves into two equally unappealing factions: a party of the past, represented by the Virginians who, as chaos closed in around them, went on fondly recounting the feud between Jefferson and Adams; and a party of the future, represented by Ovid Bolus (and Beverley Tucker and George Fitzhugh, we might add), who contributed to that chaos by severing all ties with the past and anxiously pursuing a secular millennium.

Between them these grim alternatives would seem to crowd out any possibility for an optimistic resolution to Baldwin's narrative. And yet such resolutions were almost a generic requirement in the tradition of southwestern humor, reflecting no doubt the placid, whiggish meliorism of the minds that created it. Longstreet, for example, concluded "The Fight," the best-known of his *Georgia Scenes*, by assuring his readers that "thanks to the Christian religion, to schools, colleges, and benevolent associations, such scenes of barbarism and cruelty as that which I have just been describing are now of rare occurrence."[13] Thus Baldwin, following Longstreet's precedent, provides near the end of his book a similar piece of assurance in a sketch devoted to the career of a fellow Alabama lawyer, "The Hon. Francis Strother." This paragon, we are told, "a gentleman of the Old School with the energy of the

13. Augustus Baldwin Longstreet, *Georgia Scenes* (1835; rpr. Atlanta, 1971), 64.

New," managed as commissioner of state banks of Alabama to "bring order out of chaos," balancing accounts, tracking down debtors, penetrating legal mazes of all sorts, and thus restoring the solvency and honor of the state (250, 262). The triumph of Strother is in a sense the triumph of the legal-republican worldview, confirmation of the old-time lawyer's boundless confidence in himself and his discipline. Thus was Baldwin able to conclude his account of moral anarchy on the frontier with an incongruously sanguine ending, seeming to promise Alabama's comfortable, nearly inevitable progress toward civilized order.

Yet it seems unlikely, given what we have seen of Baldwin's habits of thought, that he was entirely convinced by his own effort to honor generic convention. Francis Strother was no doubt admirable, but he was, of course, only one man, evidently the sole embodiment of virtue in a moral wasteland. And as the personification of an equilibrium between old and new, he is almost by definition a transitional figure, fixed inescapably in a particular moment of time. Like his republican ancestors, Baldwin had an understanding of civil life in which the passing of time, the transitoriness of any social moment, figured prominently. He understood American history as a typological cycle in which the country, as it moved westward, replicated over and over the stages of social development: "the savage disappearing—the frontier-man following on to a further border—that border, like the horizon, widening and stretching out towards the sinking sun, as we go on;—then the rude settlement, *now* the improved neighborhood with its schoolhouses and churches; the log cabin giving way to the mansion,—the wilderness giving way to the garden and the farm" (251). This progress is at all times represented, spatially and synchronically, by the country itself: the frontier, wherever that may be, shows the earliest stage of social development, the eastern seaboard the latest.[14] Thus "the Bostonian looks down upon the Virginian—the Virginian upon the Ten-

14. As George Dekker has shown, this "stadialist model" of progress was widely accepted in Anglo-American thought of the nineteenth century and provided the structure of its most characteristic narrative form, the historical romance. See *American Historical Romance*, 73–98.

nessean—the Tennessean on the Alabamian—the Alabamian on the Mississippian—the Mississippian on the Louisianian—the Louisianian on the Texian—the Texian on New Mexico—and, we suppose, New Mexico on Pandemonium" (223–24). Virginia was once the West, and even Alabama is merely "a full ante-type of California, in all except the gold" (84). Thus if there is always a dynamic and dangerous frontier, then there is also a decaying world left behind—the world of the decrepit and helpless Virginians, the world Baldwin himself had to leave behind to make his fortune. And presumably there is always, poised between them, a moment of virtuous equilibrium like the one created in Alabama by Francis Strother. Simply to state Baldwin's historical view in plain terms is to see its essential pessimism. That moment of equipoise is a transitory stage, a pause for breath between chaos and decay. Francis Strother, whatever his virtue, is undermined and rendered ironic by the historical process in which he figures. Do we take him as the heroic personification of virtues otherwise lost? Then Strother is a second John Randolph, a quixotic figure at war with his age, a self-consciously futile symbol of resistance to the entropic phase of republican history. Like Randolph of Roanoke, he is a powerfully articulated protest against the passage of time and the ephemerality of virtue, but he offers no solution to the problem. Ovid Bolus, Baldwin tells us, was not defeated or reformed; he simply disappeared one day, having moved farther west. He awaits us, no doubt, in California. He and his kin are legion, and the westering principle which Bolus represents—the idea of repudiating origins, fleeing history, lighting out for the territory—will always leave behind it a series of Virginias, drained of vitality, of material and cultural resources, abandoned by its most promising citizens, who must, no less than Bolus himself, follow the frontier in search of prosperity. Baldwin's historical vision almost completely undermines the hopeful narrative resolution of *The Flush Times,* translating the cautious, eighteenth-century optimism of John Taylor into the modern despair of John Randolph.

And yet by no means does *The Flush Times of Alabama and Mississippi* read like a gloomy book; it bears not the slightest resemblance, for instance, to the morbid late speeches of Randolph. The reason, undoubtedly, is the strong presence in the book of Baldwin's own unflappably amused narrative voice. If he manages to apply a high gloss of social optimism to his chronicle of depravity, he does it not by recounting the exploits of Francis Strother but by placing on display his own unfailingly urbane voice and the well-ordered mind it reflects. For Baldwin's is the most distinctive narrative voice in the tradition of southwestern humor; indeed, many students of that tradition, valuing frontier humor according to the amount of space it concedes to vernacular speech, have found this voice to be the major flaw in Baldwin's work, the thing that consigns him—compared with someone like George Washington Harris—permanently to the second string. The objection is essentially political; Baldwin, evidently, was at best enthralled to British (that is, un-American) standards of literary excellence; at worst he was a veritable enemy of democracy harboring (as one treatment of Baldwin suggests) an "obvious alignment with patrician values."[15] In truth, Baldwin was not hostile to democracy, nor was he particularly sympathetic to "patrician values," whatever those might be. But he did, I think, understand his literary voice to have political significance, and he made the most of it in *The Flush Times*.

What are the characteristics of the narrative voice that dominates and unifies the book? Baldwin's style, like his legal and political principles, seems in many ways a survival of the eighteenth century. Like his model Joseph Addison, Baldwin prefers periodic and balanced sentences, values wit and reason above genius and originality, and seeks principally to inform, persuade, and amuse. He is particularly careful to circumscribe and modulate passion by the device of sustained irony. Baldwin's voice is unfailingly poised, regardless of what horror or outrage it is obliged to disclose. It displays a narrow emotional range, oscillating between judicious admiration and disdainful amusement. Baldwin never betrays shock, outrage, or despair: *nil admirari* is his policy. Baldwin calls particular attention to that style by telling us at length how he acquired it: one of the unifying narrative strands in *The Flush Times* is the story of a young lawyer's education in courtroom rhetoric. As a Virginian, he begins by explaining, he was schooled not

15. Mary Ann Wimsatt and Robert L. Phillips, "Antebellum Humor," in *The History of Southern Literature*, ed. Louis D. Rubin *et al.* (Baton Rouge, 1986), 152.

only in legal theory but in the arts of oratory as practiced by Virginia barristers: for "it is not to be denied that Virginia is the land of orators, heroes, and statesmen" (78). But Virginia oratory, like Virginia politics, has lapsed into a decadent parody of itself: "In the showy talent of oratory she has especially shone. To accomplish her in this art, the State has been turned into a debating society, and while she has been *talking* for the benefit of the nation, as she thought, the other, and, by nature, less favored States, have been *doing* for their own. Consequently what she has gained in reputation, she has lost in wealth and *material aids*" (79). Virginia lawyers, the heirs of this tradition, are wont to lace their talk—no matter the issue at hand—with references to "'gorgons, hydras, and chimeras dire,' to black cockades, blue lights, Essex juntos, the Reign of Terror, and some other mystic entities—but who or what these monsters were, I never could distinctly learn" (77). The great tradition of Virginia oratory, that is, has degenerated into a mere habit of passionate eloquence from which the substance has all but vanished. This is the oratorical tradition in which Baldwin was raised, and we see the lingering effects of this raising in "My First Appearance at the Bar." Baldwin, called on to represent the plaintiff in a slander suit, elects in his remarks to the jury to renounce "argument and common sense" in favor of "poetry and declamation . . . pathos and fiery invective": "I grew as *quotatious* as Richard Swiveller. Shakespeare suffered. I quoted, among other things of less value and aptness, 'He who steals my purse steals trash,' &c. I spoke of the woeful sufferings of my client, almost heart broken beneath the weight of the terrible persecutions of his enemy" (32). Concluding with a few insults to his opposite number, the veteran pleader "Caesar Kasm," Baldwin retires confident that he has bludgeoned his foe into submission and won a judgment for his client. But Kasm rises, choking with rage, and administers a memorable verbal thrashing, most of it couched as a lesson in rhetoric. "I find it difficult, gentlemen," the experienced barrister begins, "to reply to any part of the young man's effort, except his argument, which is the smallest part in compass, and next to his pathos, the most amusing. His figures are some of them quite good, and have been so considered by the best judges for the last thousand years" (37). On and on Kasm goes, mercilessly flaying his opponent's high-flown rhetoric and at last producing, to the young lawyer's horror, a poem Baldwin once wrote to a young lady, subsequently published against his will by a local paper. As the jurors—"who have about as much idea or respect for poetry, as for witchcraft"—howl with laughter, and even the judge is forced to conceal his chuckles behind a coughing fit, Kasm proceeds to read Baldwin's poetic effort aloud, pausing occasionally for commentary and exegesis (42). Finally, the boy can stand it no longer; he rises and dashes out of the courtroom, his own verse and the merriment of the crowd ringing in his ears. His client, we learn, was able to secure a new trial on grounds of incompetent representation.

"My First Appearance at the Bar," one of the funniest pieces in Baldwin's book, is in part a common story of a novice's maiden flight. But it makes a point as well, for young Baldwin learns a lesson from the experience. "Reader!" he explains, "I eschewed *genius* from that day"—he learned, that is, from his drubbing at the hands of old Kasm, a new language, pragmatic in design, in which reason, learning, and measured irony replace pathos and passion (45).

This new language Baldwin has learned is the rhetorical equivalent of the ethic he advocates in *The Flush Times*. For the degeneracy of Virginia rhetoric is a telling indicator of the state's political and moral decline, even as Ovid Bolus' rhetoric, his own flights of imagination, indicate the degeneracy of Alabama. The elegant but functional language Baldwin learned by harsh experience is the equivalent of the third alternative that has been posited between those poles, the alternative represented by Francis Strother. It is not mere rhetoric, that is, but the outward and visible sign of a condition of mind. It is the language, we might say, of republican virtue. Consider, as an example, the first paragraph of the book: "And what history of that halcyon period, ranging from the year of Grace, 1835, to 1837; that golden era, when shin-plasters were the sole currency; when bank-bills were 'as thick as Autumn leaves in Vallambrosa,' and credit was a franchise— what history of those times would be complete, that left out the name of Ovid Bolus? As well write the biography of Prince Hal, and forbear all mention of Falstaff. In law phrase, the thing would be a 'deed without a name,' and void; a most unpardonable *casus omissus*" (1). Most of Baldwin's stylistic mannerisms are present here. There is, to begin with, a habit of allusion: obviously we are hearing the voice of a well-read man, quick to supply the appropriate literary or historical reference for the occasion. Horace, Shakespeare, Swift, Burke, and Rousseau all make their appearances in *The Flush Times*, as do many other figures of British and classical history. Nor did the author mind adverting, for comic or descriptive effect, to the legal jargon that formed such a large part of his intellectual equipment. This habit of allusion is pervasive enough that the most recent editor of *The Flush Times* appends fifteen pages of explanatory notes to the text. Clearly we are hearing from a broadly learned and well-read man.

Too, Baldwin's prose, in this passage and generally, reveals a hardy and orderly intelligence. His preference for the periodic sentence and his tendency to interrupt direct statements with parenthetical clarifications indicate the lawyer's concern for order and scrupulous accuracy. Further, as anyone knows who has read much of Baldwin, he has a pronounced affinity for the long sentence, sometimes very long: the first one in the passage is a fairly mild example. This mannerism is revealing as well, for (as any writer knows who has watched his own long sentences collapse like soufflés) it takes a powerful ordering intelligence to do what Baldwin does routinely: construct an elegant sentence half a page long.

The voice Baldwin creates is above all an instrument for judging, which was, by the way, his profession in the years after his literary career. It is a voice capable of lionizing Strother while still meticulously pointing out his few flaws and of revealing the frightening moral significance of Ovid Bolus while never seeming to be more than amused by his antics. It aims for balance, accuracy, and dispassionate assessment; it avoids, above all, anything resembling passion. The mind revealed by this voice is powerful, learned, disciplined by legal and literary study; it is unbiased, independent, and unafraid to speak the truth. Baldwin's style, that is, is an ideal representation of the old-fashioned legal-republican mind.

The effect of Baldwin's Addisonian style is, of course, to distance him from his subject, to identify him as the citizen of some better world, though inexplicably set down in Alabama. But more important, it also distances him from his own moral revulsion at Alabama. When in the midst of his philippic against Ovid Bolus, the personification of all he abhors, the author pauses to lay out a half-page-long sequence of parenthetical expressions, to invoke Shakespeare's history plays, and to deploy, for comic effect, a bit of legal Latin, he is deliberately controlling and directing his outrage. In effect, he places a barrier between his moral indignation and its object. The barrier is one of decorum, of literary form. Baldwin's elaborate style serves the same purpose served in poetry, according to John Crowe Ransom, by such formal constraints as meter and generic convention: "The formal tradition intends to preserve the artist from the direct approach to his object. Behind the tradition is probably the sense that the direct approach is perilous to the artist, and may be fatal." [16] So it is with Baldwin, who senses that to give vent to his outrage at Alabama would be to surrender to the principle Alabama represents: the romantic principle of the private will and the ungoverned heart. Baldwin writes an eighteenth-century prose, we might say, because he must not write a nineteenth-century prose; to lapse into the idiom of his own time and place would be, as Ransom suggests, not just perilous but actually fatal to his purpose.

It is for this reason that Baldwin must place his own voice so near the center of his work, for his voice represents the principle his book ends by advocating, the one he hopes will contain the spirit of Ovid Bolus and restore virtue to the republic. The rhetoric of republican virtue, if Baldwin can maintain it with sufficient skill, may fully and permanently embody that principle. Baldwin's narrative voice is virtually a character in *The Flush Times*, a character who stands above the fray, never astonished, never outraged, but always entertained by the antics going on below. So long as he maintains that poise, we are encouraged to hope for the preservation of, if not order, then the idea of order, in Alabama, in the South, in the republic.

In *The Flush Times* Baldwin admits that he cannot trace the lineage of Ovid Bolus and all he represents. *Party Leaders*, published just one year later, may be thought of as an effort to discover that lineage, to un-

16. John Crowe Ransom, "Forms and Citizens," in *Selected Essays of John Crowe Ransom*, ed. Thomas Daniel Young and John Hindle (Baton Rouge, 1984), 61.

derstand, by recounting its recent history, the pass which American politics had reached in the 1850s. And it is an effort as well to test his mind and language against the confusions of that age—here presented directly rather than metaphorically. In one sense the book is easy to summarize. It recounts the history of American politics from the Revolution to the present by telling the stories of five leading figures: Alexander Hamilton, Thomas Jefferson, John Randolph, Andrew Jackson, and Henry Clay. The book is meant, Baldwin says, as a celebration of American heroes, an exemplary history meant to remind Americans of their glorious heritage. And yet anyone who reads *Party Leaders* may be excused for wondering just what became of this intention in the book itself because *Party Leaders* is largely a narrative of decline. Baldwin begins, to be sure, with a celebration of the American Revolution and of the even greater triumph achieved in 1787 in Philadelphia. But this moment is the Golden Age of the republic, and it can only be followed by declension.

In fact, Baldwin telegraphs the gloomy nature of his account in his title. A book called *Party Leaders* could only be a record of error, for party was in republican theory a bad thing, institutionalizing the great evil of "faction." The very existence of parties showed that a politics of private and competing interests had replaced the old ideal of a unified public good; the presence in America of "party leaders" was a disturbing sign that the spirit of Ovid Bolus had begun to gather strength.

Thus after briefly celebrating the first moments of American political life, Baldwin comes to his real beginning, the tragedy that begins history as we know it. He begins his account, appropriately, with the struggle between Jefferson and Hamilton in the 1790s, out of which was born the first American party system. Baldwin regards this event almost literally as America's fall from grace, the moment when death entered the world of national politics. Baldwin's rendering of this episode clarifies his refinement of the Old Republican position, for despite his Virginian background and more or less Jeffersonian sympathies, he blames Jefferson more than Hamilton for this transformation. Baldwin's Alexander Hamilton is—until his very last act—an eminently practical man, completely devoted to the American Union and willing to back whatever measures will tend to preserve it. Though possessed of strong opinions and able to express them forcefully, Hamilton is in the end prepared to compromise in the interest of political unity. Jefferson, in contrast, is too much of a theorist to be a wholly effective politician—is too devoted to republicanism, we might say, to be a good republican. He finally cares more for his private vision of republican virtue than for the American Union which must embody that virtue. Republicanism—which properly made self-sacrifice and public-spiritedness the foundations of citizenship—ironically led Jefferson to a kind of narcissistic withdrawal from public commitment in favor of his own pet theories. As George Washington's administration began to follow the lead of Hamilton and as Jefferson became more and more a critic of the president and his measures, he began his long moral descent from the republican virtue of his youth.

The moral terms of this analysis represent in some ways a departure from those of Virginia republicanism. The great conflicts in American history, as Baldwin understands them, are not the familiar ones of country versus city, or local autonomy versus federal authority, or South versus North. Throughout *Party Leaders* he dismisses such disputes impatiently, regarding them as trivial occasions of self-indulgent political quarreling. Baldwin understands the disputes of American politics in terms of a very simple moral dichotomy: the virtuous politician is the one who places the public interest above all others; the vicious politician ignores that interest in favor of some private vision of truth.

These are the terms that work throughout *Party Leaders*. Baldwin regards his next "leader," John Randolph, as a complex figure who comprehends both sides of the moral dichotomy. In his quixotic withdrawal from practical politics, the great Virginia eccentric represents the personalism, the romanticism, which Baldwin would warn us against. But in his selfless devotion to Virginia, he is a model of public-spiritedness. The author wishes that Randolph had loved all America so selflessly but acknowledges that at least he loved Virginia in the way that a patriot ought to love his country. Andrew Jackson, however, is almost wholly unredeemed, a man with no regard for the past and little for present-day politics of give and take. He is the central figure of a cult of personality; he attempts to rule the country by the authority of his personal charisma, with no regard for the antique notion of the public good. Jackson's opposite is Henry Clay, the great compromiser and quintessential Whig whose concern, throughout a long career, was the preservation of the American Union. A Virginia lawyer who came west and prospered, a gentleman of the old school with the energy of the new, Clay is for Baldwin the personification of republican virtue.

Though Baldwin finds men to admire—Hamilton to a degree and Henry Clay to a greater one—the generally gloomy tone of his beginning continues to control the work to the end. Though a Hamilton or a Clay may exemplify virtue by advocating the cause of the nation itself rather than some fragment of it, these heroes are apparently destined to be overwhelmed by their enemies. Significantly, Baldwin dwells on the heroic deaths of both Hamilton and Clay, making important scenes of them. Both men, for Baldwin, were in effect struck down by their moral inferiors. Hamilton is, of course, felled by Aaron Burr's bullet, and Baldwin gives us Fisher Ames's exclamation: "My heart grows liquid as I speak, and I pour it forth like water." [17] Clay, exhausted by his last great effort to save the Union with the Compromise 1850, dies in his bed, and Baldwin himself gives the eulogy: "And thou art gone from our midst, gallant Harry Clay! and the world seems drearier than before" (368). By contrast, the author barely remembers to mention that Jefferson and Jackson have likewise passed on. In a certain sense, for Baldwin, they had not; their politics, a politics of romantic, narcissistic individualism, continued to govern the country and was now on the verge of destroying it.

In what sense, then, was this bleak record of decline meant to be celebratory or exemplary? What purpose was the book meant to serve? We can begin to find an answer, I believe, by thinking of *Party Leaders* in the way we have long since become accustomed to think of the classic works of southwestern humor, including Baldwin's: we need to think of it as a text energized by a tension between narrative action and narrative voice. The plot of the history is indeed a record of na-

17. Joseph Glover Baldwin, *Party Leaders: Sketches of Thomas Jefferson, Alex'r Hamilton, Andrew Jackson, Henry Clay, John Randolph of Roanoke* (New York, 1855), 69. Hereafter cited in the text by page number.

tional decline, which ought to induce gloom in all American readers; but the narrative voice—as in many of the works of southwestern humor—pushes us in the other direction. Thus the description I have given of *Party Leaders* is accurate and yet—as with my summary of *The Flush Times*—curiously at odds with the actual experience of reading the book. Neither *seems* a gloomy work because of the strong presence of Baldwin himself in both narratives. The voice of the narrator of *Party Leaders*—essentially the same genteel, eighteenth-century voice one hears in *The Flush Times*—is the locus of hope in Baldwin's history. If Baldwin's plot tells us of the decline of republican virtue, then his own presence in his book—his learning, his moral and intellectual rigor, and above all his effort to rise above partisanship and assess matters justly—is there to tell us that such virtue has not entirely vanished; at least one virtuous republican, the one telling the story, still survives. Like an eighteenth-century lawyer, Baldwin presents himself, with his intelligence, learning, and high principle, as a man able to make sense of the chaotic American situation and perhaps impose order upon it.

Consider, for instance, Baldwin's method of characterizing his party leaders; though his moral preferences are clear throughout, he seldom presents anyone as simply good or bad. He praises his villains, sometimes extravagantly, for what he takes to be their virtues, and he is not at all reluctant to point out the flaws in his heroes. Jefferson's *Summary View of the Rights of British America*, Baldwin thinks, was a brilliant polemic, and his faith in the common man was thoroughly admirable. Hamilton's willingness to be provoked by Aaron Burr, to risk his valuable life over a matter of honor, indicates that even he was capable of a self-regarding obsession with his own dignity which was at odds with the ideal of public service. Clay was sometimes high-handed, and even Jackson had at least the virtue of boundless energy. Baldwin's portraits of all his protagonists are judicious in the extreme—so much so that sometimes we come away with a stronger impression of the historian's judiciousness than of the actual qualities of the historical figure.

Baldwin's assessment of John Adams is an example, a complex meditation, extending for several pages, on a complex figure. After describing at length Adams' "patriotism, honesty, and magnanimity," his eloquence, and his fearless contributions to the American Revolution, Baldwin begins considering the president's failings: "He was bold, but his boldness ran to rashness. He was frank, but his frankness ran into indiscretion. His confidence made him the dupe of the most transparent designs, and his suspicions alienated him from the most trustworthy. He was full of learning, and he was full of crotchets. His judgment was far from sound; yet he had such conceit of his wisdom as made him think himself nearly infallible. He was at bottom, really, a kind, generous, noble-hearted man; but his manners were so far from conciliating that they conveyed a very different impression" (55–56). The passage is typical of *Party Leaders*. If the general narrative trajectory of the book is downward, tracing the decline of virtue in America, then that impetus is often interrupted for these long and careful evaluations, many of them extending for several pages. They all display the same rhythm as the passage I quote above, a metronomic alternation of pro and con: "on the one hand—but on the other hand—and yet—but still." As he announces in his preface, Baldwin is determined "to perform his task with candor, both in the narrative and criticism, and especially in entire freedom from all partisan bias"; he means to dole out impartial justice to all the historical figures he treats (7–8). One recalls that Baldwin was at certain times in his life a judge; certainly here his narrative voice is precisely judicial, communicating an exact calibration of moral response, aimed carefully at doing justice.

To say this is to link Baldwin with other American historians of his age. Writers like William Prescott and George Bancroft were certainly more persistent and professional in plying the historian's trade, and *Party Leaders* can hardly compare with, say, *History of the Conquest of Mexico* or *The History of the United States* in scope or thoroughness. Baldwin was never more than a talented amateur in the field of history. But he shared with certain of his contemporaries, including Prescott and Bancroft, a belief that the historian might stand as an exemplary citizen, even a *de facto* leader of his country. For many nineteenth-century historians, as John Ernest has argued, "the natural statesman of the republic [was] not the advocate, but the discerner of principles, the student of history and of men: the man of letters." [18] The idea was

18. John Ernest, "The Language of Truth: Narrative Strategy in the Histories of

a common one, arising no doubt from the republican belief that history—"philosophy teaching by example"—was the great source of political wisdom. There is, potentially, a kind of elitism in this idea, even in the hands of such a committed democrat as George Bancroft. He and certain of his contemporaries believed that in their researches they had distilled the best impulses of the American people, and they claimed the authority, or tried to, to speak in behalf of those people: the people themselves were not necessarily consulted in this arrangement. And there is in this notion—again, even in the hands of such a specialist in the optative mode as Bancroft—an implicit pessimism, a deeply rooted distrust of the people left to their own devices.

Baldwin shares many of the premises of his contemporaries, but he puts them to a significantly different use. For though a Whig, he is thoroughly democratic in his historical practice; and though gloomy about the recent course of American history, he manages, in the end, a striking optimism about the nation's prospects. He does this in part by exploiting what might seem to be weaknesses in his work: its popular rather than scholarly nature and his own undoubtedly amateur status. His book, he explains in the preface, "makes no pretension to research. The events are matters of familiar history. All that the writer has attempted has been a concise narrative of the facts, grouping them together in a compact and perspicuous shape, with such reflections as seemed to him to be just and appropriate" (8). Admitting that his work may be "wanting in the sober gravity and subdued tone, by some supposed to be the only legitimate style of history," he reminds us that he has "sought to blend interest with instruction, and, especially, to make his pages attractive to young men" (8). Then comes perhaps the most remarkable admission of all: conceding that his book may seem too favorable to the men he assesses, Baldwin explains that he prefers "to err upon the side of unmerited praise than of unjust depreciation; especially where the memories of men are concerned, whom the general voice concurs in pronouncing public benefactors" (9). The claim is extraordinary: Baldwin promises not to instruct his readers but to be

---

William H. Prescott, George Bancroft, and Henry Adams" (Ph.D. dissertation, University of Virginia, 1989), 14.

instructed by them—to defer, in his assessments of historical figures, to what he takes to be the general understanding. One can scarcely imagine anything more different from either the scholarly rigor of Prescott or the cocksure partisanship of Bancroft, every page of whose *History of the United States* was said to vote for Andrew Jackson.

Now Baldwin's claim to be writing a purely popular history is in certain respects misleading, for his book is not at all bland or lacking in forceful opinion; one carries away from *Party Leaders* a strong impression of the author's mind and principles. Nor is he excessively charitable to any of his protagonists; even the best of them are subjected to withering criticism from time to time. But still the claim is interesting, and it calls attention to the principal virtue of *Party Leaders*. For though the author is well-informed and though his judgments are often persuasive—a modern student of American political history could almost certainly learn something from Baldwin—his gift really was that of pushing common knowledge and common sense to their utmost potential. If for Prescott and Bancroft the historian was an extraordinary citizen, enabled by his knowledge of the past to see contemporary problems more clearly than his fellows, then Baldwin hopes that the historian's wisdom is not so extraordinary as to be wholly beyond the average man. The fate of the republic, John Randolph said, depended not on a small elite of "orators, philosophers and statesmen" but on the people. For Baldwin the ideal of the historian as statesman is useful only if the historian's virtues can somehow be communicated to those people.

This is the point made, for instance, by Baldwin's assessment of John Adams. Here and in general, the author does not seem particularly anxious that we agree with his historical verdicts. In fact, he surrounds those verdicts with so much contradictory evidence that we are almost compelled to draw our own conclusions. The point, it seems, is to lure us into the discussion and to provide us with a rhetorical model of how such discussions must be conducted. Baldwin wants not so much to communicate a series of judgments as to make us join in the process of judging. He proposes to discover historical truth in the same way that he wants to govern the country: not by the private insights of a small elite—down that road, ultimately, one encounters Ovid Bolus—

but by a consensus of virtuous citizens. The book is indeed exemplary, just as Baldwin says. But the exemplary figure is not Alexander Hamilton or Henry Clay, or even the voice of the narrator, but the implied coalition of narrator and reader, a community of good citizens prepared to save their country. If he can bring us into this coalition, he will have democratized the "aristocratic" mind represented by his elegant prose; he will have justified the implicit optimism embodied in that voice.

In August, 1854, even before *Party Leaders* appeared, Baldwin left the South, never to return. Displaying the restlessness that characterized him throughout his life, he moved his legal practice to San Francisco. He found California to be (as he had once predicted) the fulfillment of the entropic cycle of American history anticipated by Alabama; but he also found it, in the aftermath of the gold rush, to be another legal utopia. He prospered even more than he had in the Southwest. Soon he found himself urged to run for the state supreme court—as a Democrat, his old Whig party having by now expired—and was elected in 1858.

During the Civil War, put in the ticklish position of being a southerner serving in the government of a Union state, Baldwin maintained a public neutrality while privately rooting for the Confederate cause. His son served in a Mississippi regiment and died in the conflict. In 1863, when his business affairs took him to the East, Baldwin stopped in Washington and sought permission to visit Virginia friends behind Confederate lines. This permission was denied, but in the process he did meet Abraham Lincoln, who told him that *The Flush Times of Alabama and Mississippi* was one of his favorite books.

As well it might have been, for Lincoln had also been a frontier lawyer and no doubt had many of the experiences Baldwin described. Too, Lincoln was, like Baldwin, a member of the vanishing breed of legal generalists, men educated by apprenticeship and taught a boundless confidence in the law's power to tame difficult circumstances.[19] Robert Ferguson suggests that Lincoln's famous presidential speeches

19. Ferguson, *Law and Letters*, 305–17.

were a final triumph of the old legal mind, an effort one last time to impose order on overwhelming chaos. Perhaps this is so, and yet under the duress of war that mind was transformed. Surely nothing could be further from Baldwin's infinitely judicious and ironic style than Lincoln's quasi-biblical rhetoric at Gettysburg. Surely, too, nothing could be further from Baldwin's faith in precedent as a guide to action than Lincoln's endorsement of political novelty: his impatient rejection of "the dogmas of the quiet past" and his insistence that "as our case is new, so we must think anew, and act anew." [20] And there could be no more striking departure from Baldwin's cautious progressivism than Lincoln's teleocratic politics, his promise of a "new birth of freedom," to be achieved by a radical refounding of the old American republic. In his way, Lincoln displayed a "contempt for history and historians" not much less exuberant than Ovid Bolus'. And yet the two old frontier lawyers reportedly got on well.

Baldwin returned to California in 1864 and almost immediately began work on a new book. *The Flush Times of California* was meant as a sequel to his collection of sketches about the old southern frontier. But he was unable to complete the volume; in September, 1864, he contracted tetanus and quickly died from it at the age of forty-nine. Thus he did not live to see the new birth of freedom promised by his admirer or to see the postwar period of rampant greed called—by another, later admirer—the Gilded Age. That age would have had a familiar look about it to a man who had seen Alabama and Mississippi, not to mention California, in their prime. All of them, he might have said, were merely the "ante-types" of the new American republic.

20. Abraham Lincoln, "Annual Message to Congress," December 1, 1862, in *Speeches and Writings, 1859–1865* (New York, 1989), 415.

CONCLUSION:
AFTER THE LOST WAR

In June, 1862, as northern troops menaced Richmond, the Confederate cavalry commander J. E. B. Stuart led his command on their famous four-day "reconnaissance in force" all the way around George B. McClellan's Army of the Potomac. The ride was instantly transformed into legend (as Stuart no doubt hoped it would be), but the most memorable thing about it turned out to be one of its unintended consequences, the death and impromptu burial of its only Confederate casualty. In a successful skirmish with pursuing Union troops, Captain William Latané was shot several times and killed. The dead man's brother James carried his body to a nearby plantation, hoping to bury it there. The mistress of Westwood, Catherine Brockenbrough, readily agreed, but after the grave was dug in the family cemetery and the coffin prepared, she learned (or so the story was reported) that the northern troops occupying the area would not permit the clergyman she had summoned to pass through their lines. And so, lacking the facilities for military or ecclesiastical honors, Brockenbrough and her sister-in-law Mrs. Willoughby Newton performed the Episcopal burial service themselves, assisted by slaves and—in folklore at least—young children.

The episode, immediately reported in the Richmond papers, soon inspired one of the best-known poems of the Civil War, "The Burial of Latané," by John R. Thompson, the longtime editor of the *Southern Literary Messenger*. A couple of stanzas will suffice to suggest the tone of Thompson's poem:

A little child strewed roses on his bier,
Pale roses, not more stainless than his soul,

Nor yet more fragrant than his life sincere
that blossomed with good actions, brief but whole;
The aged matron and the faithful slave
Approached with reverent feet the hero's lowly grave.

No man of God might say the burial rite
Above the "rebel"—thus declared the foe
That blanched before him in the deadly fight,
But woman's voice, in accents soft and low,
Trembling with pity, touched with pathos, read
Over his hallowed dust the ritual for the dead.[1]

Thompson's poem was issued as a broadside in Richmond before the end of the year, and it soon caught the attention of the Virginia artist William D. Washington. Washington had been attracted to military and historical subjects and to images of Southern heroism before.[2] But in Latané's story as recounted by Thompson, he found his great subject. By 1864 he had created what became his own most famous painting and surely the most famous work of art created in the Confederacy. This work, also called *The Burial of Latané,* was an instant and spectacular success: when the painting was displayed in the Confederate Capitol in Richmond, or so a persistent story goes, a bucket was placed before it, which large and enthusiastic crowds filled and refilled with monetary donations to the Confederate cause.

Despite its tragic subject, as Drew Gilpin Faust points out in a splendid "reading" of Washington's painting, the work was meant as "a contribution to southern victory."[3] It and the poem that inspired it assured southerners of their essential kinship with one another: the mourners of Latané were strangers and yet somehow not strangers at all. Both texts reminded southerners of the cowardice and perfidy of their enemies. Most important—by their highly sentimental representations of

1. John R. Thompson, "The Burial of Latané," in *The Library of Southern Literature,* Vol. XII (Atlanta, 1910), 5243.

2. See, for instance, his *Marion's Camp* (1859).

3. Drew Gilpin Faust, "Race, Gender, and Confederate Nationalism: William D. Washington's *Burial of Latané,*" in *Southern Stories: Slaveholders in Peace and War* (Columbia, Mo., 1992), 149.

Confederate martyrdom and their equally sentimental portrayals of grateful women, children, and slaves surrounding the fallen hero—they provided the image of a society fully mobilized behind its war effort. How, both texts implicitly and confidently ask, can such a people be defeated? Thus Thompson's poem ends by wiping away the tears it has so artfully summoned and imagining the day when a triumphant Virginia will look back gratefully on Latané's sacrifice. Both works were highly skillful and successful examples of war propaganda, art in the service of military victory.

It is remarkable, then, that the story of Latané became, almost instantly after the Confederate surrender, a centerpiece in the elegiac cult of the Lost Cause. The enterprising Washington arranged for his painting to be rendered as a steel engraving, copies of which were marketed throughout the region in *Southern* magazine. This engraving enjoyed, Frank Vandiver has said, "fantastic popularity," and even now many southerners can recall seeing the print displayed proudly in the parlors of their youth. The Virginia judge who bought the original painting in 1963 was summoning such memories when he remarked that "these engravings helped to hold the Southern People together as one after the war."[4]

The same image somehow expressed equally well both the high hopes of 1862 and the painful resignation of 1865. How to account for it? How did a pair of ardent Confederates, still hoping for victory, fashion so perfect a symbol for the South's postbellum culture of defeat? My impression is that the foregoing discussion of pastoral republican ideology in the South may shed some light on the question and that the success of these representations of Latané's story may tell us something about the fate of that ideology in the years after Appomattox.

Thompson's poem seems to be spoken, at the outset, by an anonymous witness of the death of Latané, perhaps a member of his troop, who recalls the event in the first person plural: "The combat raged not long, but ours the day." This voice speaks as well, of course, for the whole region: "ours" includes all southerners reading the poem. As the

4. Mark E. Neely, Jr., Harold Holzer, and Gabor S. Borritt, *The Confederate Image: Prints of the Lost Cause* (Chapel Hill, 1987), ix.

poem goes on, however, the trooper's voice recedes, the point of view seems to become that of a disembodied, omniscient narrator, and the South is represented only by the mourners at Latané's graveside: "a little child," "the aged matron and the faithful slave." The most important of these is the "matron," presumably Mrs. Newton, who reads the burial service. In Washington's painting her centrality is particularly clear: she stands between a party of slaves on one side of the open grave and a party of white women on the other, uniting them in shared grief.

The background of the action, in poem and painting, is nature itself; in this respect both artists are echoing the version of the Latané story which—rather implausibly—places his grave in the "garden" of the plantation rather than the cemetery. Thompson's poem makes extensive use of pastoral imagery, reminding us not only of the "pale blossoms" strewn by the child but also of Latané's honors, the "blossoms" of a virtuous life, and of the Prayer Book's promise of resurrection: "'Tis sown in weakness, it is raised in power." Though not a pastoral elegy in any strict sense, Thompson's poem has in common with that familiar form its use of natural imagery as a source of consolation. Washington's painting does the same thing, again even more vividly than the poem. In it only a few man-made objects are visible—Mrs. Newton's prayer book, the shovel held by one slave, Latané's cloak and saber, and the coffin on which they rest. Mrs. Newton herself stands amid the clods displaced from Latané's grave and seems almost to have risen directly from the earth; all around her is greenery, and behind her stretches a hazy but plainly rural Virginia landscape. In both texts Mrs. Newton is in effect the personification of Virginia—gendered female by a very old convention—leading her "children" in mourning.

The scene is a funeral, the occasion for mourning a past now vanished beyond recovery. And yet this fact—the irrevocable pastness of the past—is one of the sources of consolation:

> Let us not weep for him whose deeds endure,
> So young, so brave, so beautiful, he died;
> As he had wished to die; the past is sure,
> Whatever yet of sorrow may betide

Those who still linger by the stormy shore,
Change cannot harm him now, nor fortune touch him more.

Our comfort arises from knowing that Latané is now safely part of the past, that he has been granted an instantaneous and painless escape from history:

One moment on the battle's edge he stood,
Hope's halo like a helmet round his hair,
The next beheld him, dabbled in his blood,
Prostrate in death, and yet in death how fair!

In sharp contrast with the survivors, who must "linger by the stormy shore," Latané now lives in a country of immutable order ("the past is sure"), immune to the forces of history ("Change cannot harm him now"). To be sure, Thompson duly adds a final stanza in which the future is confidently invoked; but that stanza seems almost contrary in purpose to the rest of the elegy. Washington's painting, unable to invoke a future moment for comparison with the present one, delivers its elegiac message unalloyed, which may account for its relatively greater popularity and longevity.

Perhaps the implications of all of this are evident already. What we are recognizing in both poem and painting is not mere sentimentality; nor is it simply the stock "pastoral" imagery so often found in elegiac English verse (and associated with the burial of the dead by, among other things, a contemporary American phenomenon, the "rural cemetery movement"). It is the iconography of the pastoral republic, the symbolism associated with southern ideology during the fifty years before secession. If the scene depicted is meant to represent something essential about the South, then the message would seem clear enough: the South is a virtuous pastoral realm besieged by a morally inferior yet physically more powerful one (the cowardly enemy who can forbid the attendance of a "man of God"). The South—once championed by powerful heroes like Latané—is now represented only by women, children, and slaves: figures who represent moral innocence but also passivity, weakness, and helplessness.[5] The South represented in painting

5. Anne Norton has written suggestively about the antebellum southern habit of

and poem, like the South to which those artifacts were addressed, struggles to focus its attention on a promised victory but finds it difficult to escape the elegiac mode. Its best hope, a forlorn one indeed, is that some image of past virtue may be preserved—not in reality but in memory.

To recognize all of this is to begin to see how the same cluster of symbols might have served equally well the causes of southern nationhood and southern elegy. For in truth southerners had begun pronouncing elegies upon their nation almost as soon as they began to believe that they had one—think again of *The Valley of Shenandoah,* that profoundly gloomy plantation novel of 1824. Since the early nineteenth century even avid southern partisans, trying their best to lead cheers for their region, had found themselves slipping helplessly back into the old, familiar, nostalgic mode—or even, in a few cases, the apocalyptic: "Hares will hurdle in the Capitol," John Randolph had said; "Congress will liberate our slaves in twenty years." The story I have told in the foregoing pages might be summarized as the South's effort to fight free of the elegiac mode and learn to speak in suitably American, optimistic accents. That so many southerners found it impossible to do so is testimony, I believe, to the power of pastoral republican ideology, for that body of thought lent itself to no other literary mode quite so well as to the elegiac. Even Nathaniel Beverley Tucker, prophet of southern destiny, was never able to break the habit of referring to his homeland as "Old Virginia," or even "Poor Old Virginia"—adopting before Thomas Nelson Page was born the language that famous elegist of the Old South would deploy in the 1880s and 1890s.[6]

All of this may shed some light on a very old question in southern history: how was it that Confederate southerners—though proclaiming their utter determination up until the moment of surrender—accepted their defeat so quickly and quietly afterward? Why did the prolonged guerrilla resistance that might have been expected not materialize? An old but persistent theory argues that southerners must never fully have

---

identifying the region with these figures of passivity and helplessness; see *Alternative Americas,* 132–99.

6. Brugger, *Beverley Tucker,* 1.

believed in their own cause; otherwise they would not have surrendered it so readily. But this theory has never been able to account for the sacrifices Confederates made in the war: according to Shelby Foote, the South suffered a casualty rate—one man out of every four killed or disabled—almost unequaled in the recorded history of warfare.[7] But southerners' sincere belief in their national cause and their quiet acceptance of its failure may not be incompatible. Defeat, as the foregoing chapters have suggested, was an experience many southerners had imagined for themselves in considerable detail long before Lee rode forth to meet Grant at Appomattox. When it finally arrived, it must have had for many a familiar look about it. Father Abraham Ryan was able to write "The Conquered Banner," which became the South's nearly official literary interpretation of its defeat, within an hour of receiving the news from Appomattox.[8] "We have lost all but honor," southerners told one another repeatedly in the years after the surrender: exactly what they had expected to lose, and to keep. And so when postwar writers like Page tried to give an account of a virtuous, vanished past—producing nostalgic works with titles like *In Ole Virginia*, *The Old Dominion*, and *The Old South*—they were not doing anything particularly new. Like so much southern writing from before the war, these works memorialize a South whose spotless perfection—existing as it does only in memory—"change cannot harm."

Nor does the pattern disappear with Page and his contemporaries. Consider, for example, the work of the Fugitive-Agrarians who were so central to the southern literary renascence of the 1920s, 1930s, and 1940s. What will happen if we bring to the study of these writers an awareness of the pastoral republican tradition in the regional past, including, particularly, the pastoral republican will to escape history? Does not the effort of men like Ransom and Tate to revive the ideal of the pastoral republic in *I'll Take My Stand* begin to look like a familiar gesture? And does not the failure of this political effort—this engagement with history—and these writers' subsequent withdrawal

7. Foote, *Civil War*, 1040–41.
8. Gaines M. Foster, *Ghosts of the Confederacy: Defeat, the Lost Cause, and the Emergence of the New South* (New York, 1987), 36.

to the world of art seem the almost inevitable sequel? Recall what Allen Tate wrote to John Peale Bishop at the end of 1933, before the Agrarian moment was fully over—that his loyalties were owed to "the republic of letters . . . the only kind of republic I believe in, a kind of republic that can't exist in a political republic."[9] Does not the stable, iconic text postulated by New Criticism, with its capacity to contain and resolve conflict by means of irony, begin to look like that refuge from history, that country of changeless order, for which southern republicans have always searched?

Nor, though the New Criticism has now yielded place to several newer ones, have southerners altogether abandoned that search. I glance to my left as I write this and discover on my shelves, in the general vicinity of *I'll Take My Stand*, the following more recent titles: *The Lasting South, The Everlasting South, The Enduring South, The Prevailing South*, and *Why the South Will Survive*. Indeed, the pastoral republican tradition, even in the relentlessly practical form articulated by John Taylor, displays a remarkable persistence, as witness the career of the Kentucky writer and farmer Wendell Berry, whose novels, poems, and essays (on literature, politics, and agriculture) constitute one long negotiation between "ideas and substances." The continuing appeal of pastoral republican ideas in the modern age is a fascinating subject, and one that might reward substantial investigation. It is, however, a subject for another day.

But as for the five Virginians whose careers we have followed in the present study, the pattern seems clear enough. Perhaps we can summarize it by recalling two provocative statements made by two of their self-conscious modern heirs. Allen Tate observed in 1931 that "the significance of the Southern way of life, in my time, is failure." And Robert Penn Warren, the brilliant boy whom Tate introduced to the Fugitive circle, famously asserted that "poetry is the little myth we write, while history is the big myth we live, and in our living constantly

---

9. Allen Tate to John Peale Bishop, December 23, 1933, in *The Republic of Letters in America: The Correspondence of John Peale Bishop and Allen Tate*, ed. Thomas Daniel Young and John Hindle (Lexington, 1981), 94.

remake." [10] The Virginians, fearing to acknowledge that the significance of their own "southern experience" might indeed be "failure," all did their best to write a new myth for their region. All of them ended by helplessly living an old one.

10. Allen Tate to John Peale Bishop, early June, 1931, *ibid.*, 34; Robert Penn Warren, *Brother to Dragons: A Tale in Verse and Voices* (New York, 1953), xii.

BIBLIOGRAPHY

Adair, Douglass. "Rumbold's Dying Speech, 1685, and Jefferson's Last Words on Democracy, 1826." In *Fame and the Founding Fathers: Essays by Douglass Adair*, edited by H. Trevor Colbourn. New York, 1974.

Adams, Henry. *John Randolph*, Boston, 1898.

Appleby, Joyce. *Capitalism and a New Social Order: The Republican Vision of the 1790's.* New York, 1984.

———. *Liberalism and Republicanism in the Historical Imagination.* Cambridge, Mass., 1992.

Bailyn, Bernard. *The Ideological Origins of the American Revolution.* Cambridge, Mass., 1967.

Bain, Robert, Joseph M. Flora, and Louis D. Rubin, Jr., eds. *Southern Writers: A Biographical Dictionary.* Baton Rouge, 1979.

Bakker, Jan. *Pastoral in Antebellum Southern Romance.* Baton Rouge, 1989.

Baldwin, Joseph Glover. *The Flush Times of Alabama and Mississippi: A Series of Sketches by Joseph G. Baldwin.* Introduction by James Justus. 1853; rpr. Baton Rouge, 1987.

———. *The Flush Times of California.* Edited by Richard E. Amacher and George W. Polhemus. Athens, Ga., 1966.

———. *Party Leaders: Sketches of Thomas Jefferson, Alex'r Hamilton, Andrew Jackson, Henry Clay, John Randolph, of Roanoke.* New York, 1855.

Banning, Lance. *The Jeffersonian Persuasion: Evolution of a Party Ideology.* Ithaca, 1978.

Baritz, Loren. *City on a Hill: A History of Ideas and Myths in America.* New York, 1964.

Baym, Nina. "Melodramas of Beset Manhood: How Theories of American Fiction Exclude Women Authors." *American Quarterly*, XXXIII (1981), 123–39.

Benton, Thomas Hart. *Thirty Years' View: A History of the Working of the*

American Government for Thirty Years, from 1820 to 1850. New York, 1854.

Bercovitch, Sacvan. *The American Jeremiad*. Madison, Wisc., 1978.

———. "How the Puritans Won the American Revolution." *Massachusetts Review*, XVII (1976), 597–630.

Bradford, M. E. *Generations of the Faithful Heart: On the Literature of the South*. La Salle, Ill., 1983.

Brown, Roger H. *The Republic in Peril: 1812*. New York, 1971.

Bruce, Dickson D., Jr. *The Rhetoric of Conservatism: The Virginia Convention of 1829–30 and the Conservative Tradition in the South*. San Marino, Calif., 1982.

———. *Violence and Culture in the Antebellum South*. Austin, 1980.

Bruce, William Cabell. *John Randolph of Roanoke, 1773–1833*. 2 vols. New York, 1922.

Brugger, Robert J. *Beverley Tucker: Heart over Head in the Old South*. Baltimore, 1974.

Burke, Kenneth. *The Philosophy of Literary Form: Studies of Symbolic Action*. Baton Rouge, 1941.

Butterfield, Herbert. *The Whig Interpretation of History*. New York, 1965.

Byrd, William. "Letter to Lord Orrery." In *Southern Writing, 1585–1920*, edited by Richard Beale Davis, C. Hugh Holman, and Louis D. Rubin, Jr. New York, 1970.

Calhoun, John. "Speech on the Reception of the Abolition Petitions." In *Union and Liberty: The Political Philosophy of John Calhoun*, edited by Ross Lence. Indianapolis, 1992.

Carlyle, Thomas. "Characteristics." In *Critical and Miscellaneous Essays*, Vol. III. New York, 1900.

———. "The Present Time." In *Latter-Day Pamphlets*. New York, 1901.

Colbourn, H. Trevor. *The Lamp of Experience: Whig History and the Intellectual Origins of the American Revolution*. Chapel Hill, 1965.

Connelly, Thomas, and Barbara L. Bellows. *God and General Longstreet: The Lost Cause and the Southern Mind*. Baton Rouge, 1982.

Cooper, William J., Jr. *Liberty and Slavery: Southern Politics to 1860*. New York, 1983.

Craven, Avery O. *The Growth of Southern Nationalism, 1848–1861*. Baton Rouge, 1953.

Davis, Richard Beale. *Intellectual Life in Jefferson's Virginia, 1790–1830*. Chapel Hill, 1964.

Dawidoff, Robert. *The Education of John Randolph*. New York, 1979.

Dekker, George. *The American Historical Romance*. Cambridge, Eng., 1987.

Donald, David. "Died of Democracy." In *Why the North Won the Civil War*, edited by David Donald. Baton Rouge, 1960.

―――. "The Proslavery Argument Reconsidered." *Journal of Southern History*, XXXVII (1971), 4–18.

―――. "Toward a Reconsideration of Abolitionists." In *Lincoln Reconsidered*. New York, 1961.

Dowling, William C. *Poetry and Ideology in Revolutionary Connecticut*. Athens, Ga., 1990.

Drayton, Michael. "To the Virginian Voyage." In *The Golden Hind: An Anthology of Elizabethan Prose and Poetry*, edited by Roy Lamson and Hallett Smith. New York, 1942.

Dudley, Theodore, ed. *Letters of John Randolph to a Young Relative, Embracing a Series of Years, from Early Youth, to Mature Manhood*. Philadelphia, 1834.

Eaton, Clement. *A History of the Old South*. New York, 1949.

―――. *The Mind of the Old South*. Baton Rouge, 1964.

Emerson, Ralph Waldo. *Lectures and Biographical Sketches*. Boston, 1911. Vol. X of *The Complete Works of Ralph Waldo Emerson*.

Ernest, John. "The Language of Truth: Narrative Strategy in the Histories of William H. Prescott, George Bancroft, and Henry Adams." Ph.D. dissertation, University of Virginia, 1989.

Faust, Drew Gilpin. *The Creation of Confederate Nationalism: Ideology and Identity in the Civil War South*. Baton Rouge, 1988.

―――. *The Sacred Circle: The Dilemma of the Intellectual in the Old South, 1840–1860*. Baltimore, 1977.

―――. *Southern Stories: Slaveholders in Peace and War*. Columbia, Mo., 1992.

Ferguson, Robert A. *Law and Letters in American Culture*. Cambridge, Mass., 1984.

Fisher, Philip. *Hard Facts: Setting and Form in the American Novel*. New York, 1987.

Fitzhugh, George. *Cannibals All! or, Slaves Without Masters*. Edited by C. Vann Woodward. Cambridge, Mass., 1960.

―――. "The Revolutions of 1776 and 1861 Contrasted." *Southern Literary Messenger*, XXXV (1863), 718–26.

―――. *Sociology for the South; or, The Failure of Free Society*. Richmond, 1854.

―――. "Southern Thought." In *The Ideology of Slavery: Proslavery Thought in the Antebellum South, 1830–1860*, edited by Drew Gilpin Faust. Baton Rouge, 1981.

————. "The Valleys of Virginia—The Rappahannock." *De Bow's Review*, XXVI (1859), 267–82.

Foote, Shelby. *The Civil War: Red River to Appomattox*. New York, 1974.

Ford, Lacy. "Republican Ideology in a Slave Society: The Political Economy of John C. Calhoun." *Journal of Southern History*, LIV (1988), 405–24.

Forgie, George B. *Patricide in the House Divided: A Psychological Interpretation of Lincoln and His Age*. New York, 1979.

Foster, Gaines M. *Ghosts of the Confederacy: Defeat, the Lost Cause, and the Emergence of the New South*. New York, 1987.

Garland, Hugh A. *The Life of John Randolph of Roanoke*. 2 vols. New York, 1850.

Geertz, Clifford. *The Interpretation of Cultures*. New York, 1973.

Genovese, Eugene D. *The World the Slaveholders Made: Two Essays in Interpretation*. New York, 1969.

Gilmore, Michael T. *American Romanticism and the Marketplace*. Chicago, 1985.

Grammer, G. C. "The Failure of Free Society." *De Bow's Review*, XIX (1855), 29–38.

Gray, Richard. *Writing the South: Ideas of an American Region*. Cambridge, Eng., 1986.

Greenberg, Kenneth S. *Masters and Statesmen: The Political Culture of American Slavery*. Baltimore, 1985.

Greene, Jack P. *Landon Carter: An Inquiry into the Personal Values and Social Imperatives of the Eighteenth-Century Virginia Gentry*. Charlottesville, 1965.

————. *Pursuits of Happiness: The Social Development of Early Modern British Colonies and the Formation of American Culture*. Chapel Hill, 1988.

Gura, Philip. "Turning Our World Upside Down: Reconceiving Early American Literature." *American Literature*, LXIII (1991), 104–12.

Hartz, Louis. *The Liberal Tradition in America: An Interpretation of American Political Thought Since the Revolution*. New York, 1955.

Hobson, Fred. *Tell About the South: The Southern Rage to Explain*. Baton Rouge, 1983.

Holman, C. Hugh. *The Roots of Southern Writing*. Athens, Ga., 1972.

Holt, Michael F. *The Political Crisis of the 1850's*. New York, 1978.

Hubbell, Jay B. *The South in American Literature*. Durham, 1954.

Hughes, Henry. *A Treatise on Sociology, Theoretical and Practical*. Philadelphia, 1854.

Hundley, Daniel R. *Social Relations in Our Southern States*. Edited by William J. Cooper, Jr. Baton Rouge, 1979.

Jamieson, T. John. "Conservatism's Metaphysical Vision: Barbey d'Aurevilly on Joseph de Maistre." *Modern Age*, XXIX (1985), 28–37.

Jefferson, Thomas. *Writings*. Edited by Merrill Peterson. New York, 1984.

Johnson, Gerald W. *Randolph of Roanoke: A Political Fantastic*. New York, 1929.

Jordan, Winthrop D. *White over Black: American Attitudes Toward the Negro, 1550–1812*. Chapel Hill, 1968.

Kennedy, John Pendleton. *Swallow Barn; or, A Sojourn in the Old Dominion*. 1851; rpr. Baton Rouge, 1986.

Kermode, Frank. Introduction to *English Pastoral Poetry: From the Beginnings to Marvell*. New York, 1972.

Kirk, Russell. *The Conservative Mind: From Burke to Eliot*. Chicago, 1972.

———. *John Randolph of Roanoke: A Study in American Politics*. 3rd ed. Indianapolis, 1978.

Kreyling, Michael. *Figures of the Hero in Southern Narrative*. Baton Rouge, 1986.

Levin, David. *History as Romantic Art: Bancroft, Prescott, Motley, and Parkman*. Stanford, 1959.

Lienesch, Michael. *New Order of the Ages: Time, the Constitution, and the Making of Modern American Political Thought*. Princeton, 1988.

Lincoln, Abraham. *Speeches and Writings, 1859–1865*. New York, 1989.

Linden, Fabian. "Economic Democracy in the Slave South." *Journal of Negro History*, XXXI (1946), 140–89.

Longstreet, Augustus Baldwin. *Georgia Scenes*. 1835; rpr. Atlanta, 1971.

Lynn, Kenneth S. *Mark Twain and Southwestern Humor*. Boston, 1959.

Lytle, Andrew Nelson. "John Taylor of Caroline." In *From Eden to Babylon: The Social and Political Essays of Andrew Nelson Lytle*. Washington, D.C., 1990.

Mannheim, Karl. "The Meaning of Conservatism." In *Essays on Sociology and Social Psychology*. London, 1953.

Marx, Leo. *The Machine in the Garden: Technology and the Pastoral Idea in America*. New York, 1964.

McCardell, John. *The Idea of a Southern Nation: Southern Nationalists and Southern Nationalism, 1830–1860*. New York, 1979.

McCoy, Drew. *The Elusive Republic: Political Economy in Jeffersonian America*. Chapel Hill, 1980.

McDonald, Forrest. *Novus Ordo Seclorum: The Intellectual Origins of the Constitution*. Lawrence, Kan., 1985.

Meyers, Marvin. *The Jacksonian Persuasion: Politics and Belief*. 2nd ed. Stanford, 1960.

Miller, Perry. "From the Covenant to the Revival." In *Nature's Nation*. Cambridge, Mass., 1967.

————. *The Life of the Mind in America: From the Revolution to the Civil War*. New York, 1965.

Mudge, Eugene Tenbroeck. *The Social Philosophy of John Taylor of Caroline: A Study in Jeffersonian Democracy*. New York, 1939.

Neely, Mark E., Jr., Harold Holzer, and Gabor S. Borritt. *The Confederate Image: Prints of the Lost Cause*. Chapel Hill, 1987.

Nisbet, Robert. *The Sociological Tradition*. New York, 1966.

Norton, Anne. *Alternative Americas: A Reading of Antebellum Political Culture*. Chicago, 1986.

Oakes, James. *The Ruling Race: A History of American Slaveholders*. New York, 1982.

O'Brien, Michael, ed. *All Clever Men, Who Make Their Way: Critical Discourse in the Old South*. Fayetteville, 1982.

————. *Rethinking the South: Essays in Intellectual History*. Baltimore, 1988.

O'Brien, Michael, and David Moltke-Hansen, eds. *Antebellum Charleston*. Knoxville, 1986.

Owsley, Frank L. *Plain Folk of the Old South*. Introduction by Grady McWhiney. 1949; rpr. Baton Rouge, 1982.

Pangle, Thomas L. *The Spirit of Modern Republicanism: The Moral Vision of the American Founders and the Philosophy of Locke*. Chicago, 1988.

Parks, Edd Winfield, ed. *Southern Poets: Representative Selections, with Introduction, Bibliography, and Notes*. 1936; rpr. New York, 1970.

Pease, Donald. *Visionary Compacts*. Madison, Wisc., 1985.

Pocock, J. G. A. *The Machiavellian Moment: Florentine Political Thought and the Atlantic Republican Tradition*. Princeton, 1975.

————. *Politics, Language and Time: Essays on Political Thought and History*. New York, 1971.

Poe, Edgar Allan. "George Balcombe." *Southern Literary Messenger*, III (1837), 49–58.

Poore, Bejamin Perley. *Perley's Reminiscences of Sixty Years in the National Metropolis*. 2 vols. Philadelphia, 1886.

Randolph, John. "Speech Against War With England." In *Randolph of Roanoke*, by Russell Kirk. Indianapolis, 1978.

Ransom, John Crowe. "Forms and Citizens." In *Selected Essays of John Crowe Ransom*, edited by Thomas Daniel Young and John Hindle. Baton Rouge, 1984.

————. "Reconstructed but Unregenerate." In Twelve Southerners, *I'll Take My Stand: The South and the Agrarian Tradition*. New York, 1930.

Reising, Russell. *The Unusable Past: Theory and the Study of American Literature*. New York, 1986.

Ridgely, J. V. *Nineteenth Century Southern Literature*. Lexington, 1980.

Risjord, Norman K. *The Old Republicans: Southern Conservatism in the Age of Jefferson*. New York, 1965.

Rodgers, Daniel. "Republicanism: The Career of a Concept." *Journal of American History*, LXXIX (1992), 11–38.

Rubin, Louis D., In *The Edge of the Swamp: A Study in the Literature and Society of the Old South*. Baton Rouge, 1989.

———— et al., eds. *The History of Southern Literature*. Baton Rouge, 1986.

Shalhope, Robert E. *John Taylor of Caroline: Pastoral Republican*. Columbia, S.C., 1980.

————. "Republicanism and Early American Historiography." *William and Mary Quarterly*, 3rd ser., XXXIX (1982), 334–56.

————. *The Roots of Democracy: American Thought and Culture, 1760–1800*. Boston, 1990.

————. "Toward a Republican Synthesis: The Emergence of an Understanding of Republicanism in American Historiography." *William and Mary Quarterly*, 3rd. ser., XXIX (1972), 49–80.

Shorey, Kenneth, ed. *The Collected Letters of John Randolph of Roanoke to Dr. John Brockenbrough, 1812–1833*. New Brunswick, 1988.

Simkins, Francis Butler, and Charles Pierce Roland. *A History of the South*. 4th ed. New York, 1972.

Simms, Henry H. *Life of John Taylor: The Story of a Brilliant Leader in the Early Virginia State Rights School*. Richmond, 1932.

Simpson, Lewis P. *The Brazen Face of History: Studies in the Literary Consciousness in America*. Baton Rouge, 1980.

————. *The Dispossessed Garden: Pastoral and History in Southern Literature*. 2nd ed. Baton Rouge, 1983.

————. *The Fable of the Southern Writer*. Baton Rouge, 1994.

————. *The Man of Letters in New England and the South: Essays on the History of the Literary Vocation in America*. Baton Rouge, 1973.

————. *Mind and the American Civil War: A Meditation on Lost Causes*. Baton Rouge, 1989.

Smith, Henry Nash. *Virgin Land: The American West as Symbol and Myth*. Cambridge, Mass., 1950.

Stewart, Samuel Boyd. "Joseph Glover Baldwin." Ph.D. dissertation, Vanderbilt University, 1941.

Sydnor, Charles S. *The Development of Southern Sectionalism, 1819–1848*. Baton Rouge, 1948.

Tate, Allen. *Collected Essays*. Denver, 1959.

Taylor, John. *Arator, Being a Series of Essays, Practical and Political, in Sixty-Four Numbers*. Edited by M. E. Bradford. Indianapolis, 1977.

———. *Construction Construed and Constitutions Vindicated*. Richmond, 1820.

———. *An Inquiry into the Principles and Policy of the Government of the United States*. Indianapolis, 1969.

———. *Tyranny Unmasked*. Edited by F. Thornton Miller. Indianapolis, 1992.

Taylor, William R. *Cavalier and Yankee: The Old South and American National Character*. New York, 1961.

Thompson, John R. "The Burial of Latané." In *The Library of Southern Literature*, Vol XII. Atlanta, 1910.

Thornton, J. Mills, III. *Politics and Power in a Slave Society: Alabama, 1800–1860*. Baton Rouge, 1978.

Timrod, Henry. *The Collected Poems of Henry Timrod*. Edited by Edd Winfield Parks and Aileen Wells Parks. Athens, Ga., 1965.

Tise, Larry E. *Proslavery: A History of the Defense of Slavery in America, 1701–1840*. Athens, Ga., 1987.

Tocqueville, Alexis de. *Democracy in America*. Translated by Henry Reeve. New York, 1947.

Tompkins, Jane. *Sensational Designs: The Cultural Work of American Fiction, 1790–1860*. New York, 1985.

Tucker, Beverley D. *Nathaniel Beverley Tucker: Prophet of the Confederacy, 1784–1851*. Tokyo, 1979.

Tucker, George. *The Valley of Shenandoah; or, Memoirs of the Graysons*. 1824; rpr. Chapel Hill, 1970.

Tucker, Nathaniel Beverley. *The Partisan Leader: A Tale of the Future*. 1836; rpr. Chapel Hill, 1971.

Tucker, St. George. *A Dissertation on Slavery: With a Proposal for the Gradual Elimination of It in the State of Virginia*. Philadelphia, 1796.

Tuveson, Ernest Lee. *Redeemer Nation: The Idea of America's Millennial Role*. Chicago, 1968.

Warren, Robert Penn. *Brother to Dragons: A Tale in Verse and Voices*. New York, 1953.

Weaver, Richard M. *The Southern Essays of Richard M. Weaver*. Edited by George M. Curtis III and James J. Thompson, Jr. Indianapolis, 1987.

———. *The Southern Tradition at Bay.* Edited by George Core and M. E. Bradford. New Rochelle, 1968.

Webster, Daniel. *The Works of Daniel Webster.* 2nd ed. Boston, 1853.

Whitman, Walt. *Walt Whitman: Complete Poetry and Collected Prose.* New York, 1982.

Williams, Raymond. *The Country and the City.* New York, 1973.

Wills, Garry. *Lincoln at Gettysburg: The Words That Remade America.* New York, 1992.

Wish, Harvey. *George Fitzhugh, Propagandist of the Old South.* Baton Rouge, 1943.

Wood, Gordon S. *The Creation of the American Republic, 1776–1787.* Chapel Hill, 1969.

Wood, Kirk. "The Central Theme of Southern History: Republicanism, Not Slavery, Race, or Romanticism." *Continuity,* IX (1984), 33–72.

Woodward, C. Vann. *The Burden of Southern History.* Rev. ed. Baton Rouge, 1968.

———. "George Fitzhugh, *Sui Generis.*" Introduction to *Cannibals All!* or, *Slaves Without Masters.* Cambridge, Mass., 1960.

Wyatt-Brown, Bertram. *Southern Honor: Ethics and Behavior in the Old South.* New York, 1982.

Yeats, William Butler. *Collected Poems.* New York, 1979.

———. *Reveries over Childhood and Youth.* In *The Autobiography of William Butler Yeats.* New York, 1953.

Young, Thomas Daniel, and John Hindle, eds. *The Republic of Letters in America: The Correspondence of John Peale Bishop and Allen Tate.* Lexington, 1981.

INDEX